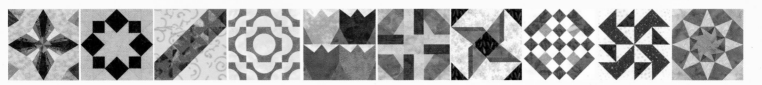

1000
ANY-SIZE
QUILT
BLOCKS

by Linda Causee and Rita Weiss

LEISURE ARTS, INC
Little Rock, Arkansas

Produced by

CREATIVE PARTNERS LLC

Production Team

Creative Directors: Jean Leinhauser
Rita Weiss
Production: Linda Causee
April McArthur

Library of Congress Control Number: 2011945915

ISBN-13/EAN: 978-1-60900-332-6

10 9 8 7 6 5 4 3 2

Contents

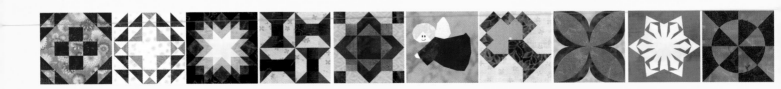

Before You Begin

Have you always wanted to make a quilt, but found drawing templates too difficult? Are you an experienced quilter who enjoys quilt making except for the drafting of patterns?

Your troubles are now over! This book and the attached CD can solve your problem.

Choose the quilt block you want, place the CD in the computer and—as if by magic—the necessary pattern will appear before you. Click on the block you want in the size that you desire and print out all of the pattern pieces needed for your quilt. If your original pattern pieces become worn or lost, just repeat the process.

There are two different kinds of blocks in this book: blocks that use templates and blocks that use foundation piecing. The CD is divided into sections that correspond to the chapters in the book. When you open the CD, you will find a folder for each chapter. In the folders for the template blocks (pages 4 to 69), you will find a diagram for each block labeled with the templates used to make the block. Also included in each folder are the necessary templates for the blocks in various sizes. In the folders for the foundation blocks (pages 70-115), you will find each block pattern (in three sizes) with numbers showing the piecing order.

The blocks on the CD are given in various sizes depending on whether they are Foundation, Four Patch, Five Patch or Nine Patch blocks. You can add additional sizes by reducing or enlarging your printer output. If you would like your blocks to be a different size, use the following guide:

Four-Patch Blocks

2" block – use 4" block, reduce 50%

6" block – use 4" block, enlarge 150%

10" block – use 4" block, enlarge 250%

14" block – use 8" block, enlarge 175%

16" block – use 8" block, enlarge 200%

Nine-Patch Blocks

3" block – use 6" block, reduce 50%

7½" block – use 3" block, enlarge 175%

10½" block – use 6" block, enlarge 175%

13½" block – use 9" block, enlarge 150%

15" block – use 6" block, enlarge 250%

Five-Patch Blocks

2½" block – use 5" block, reduce 50"

7½" block – use 5" block, enlarge 150%

12½" block – use 5" block, enlarge 250%

17½" block – use 10" block, enlarge 175%

Foundation Blocks

2" block – use 4" block, reduce 50%

3" block – use 6" block, reduce 50%

9" block – use 6" block, enlarge 150%

10" block – use 4" block, enlarge 250%

12" block – use 6" block, enlarge 200%

14" block – use 8" block, enlarge 175%

16" block – use 8" block, enlarge 200%

If you've forgotten—or if you've never learned—how to make a quilt, we've included some basic instructions on pages 116 to 128.

So get ready to enjoy a whole world of quilt making. Get ready to make a miniature quilt, a wall hanging or a full-size bed quilt. Get ready to repeat one block over and over for a quilt that will draw applause from all your friends and family, or make a quilt without repeating a block. The choice is yours, and there are lots of choices.

There are 1,000 quilt blocks waiting for you.

Four Patch Blocks

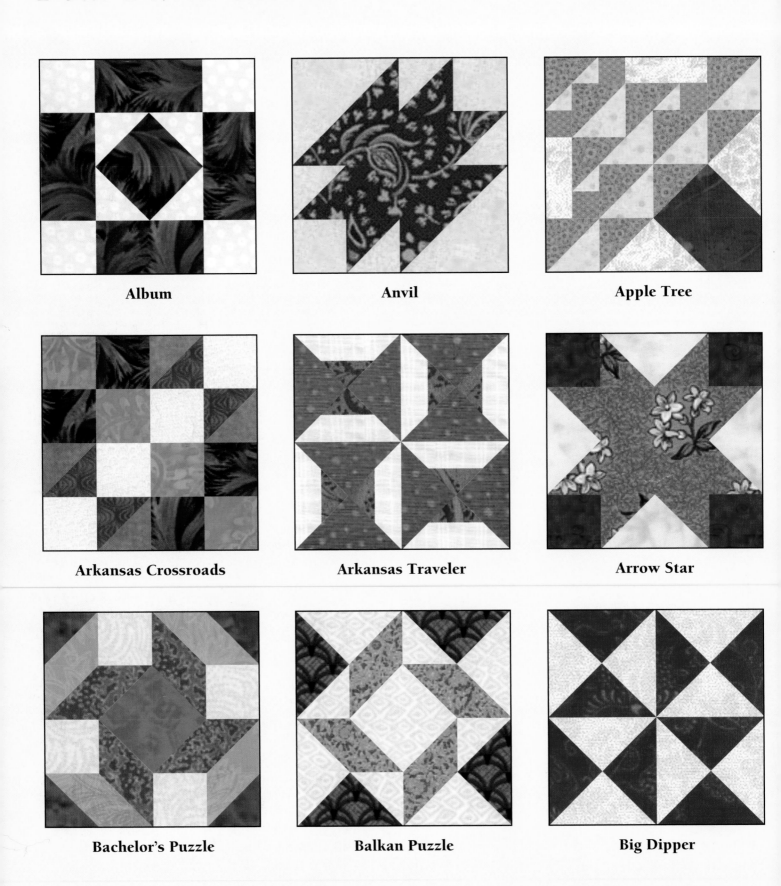

Album

Anvil

Apple Tree

Arkansas Crossroads

Arkansas Traveler

Arrow Star

Bachelor's Puzzle

Balkan Puzzle

Big Dipper

Blackford's Beauty

Blockade

Bouquet

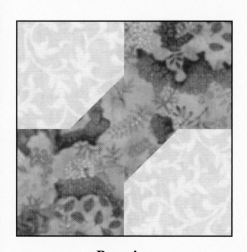

Bowties

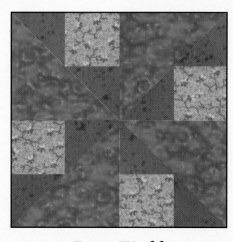

Brave World

Broken Dishes

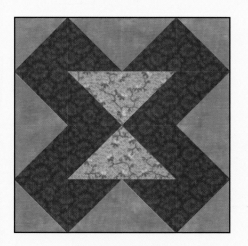

Brown Goose

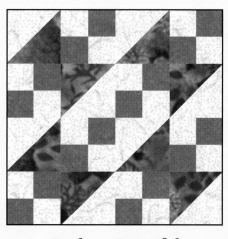

Buckeye Beautiful

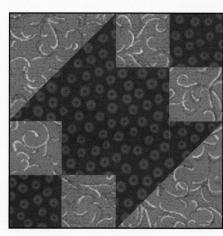

Buckeye Beauty

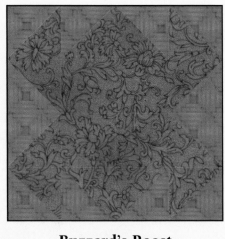

Buzzard's Roost

Cactus Basket 1

Carpenter's Wheel

Catch as you Can

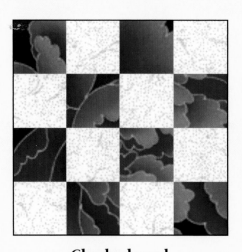

Checkerboard

Chevron

Chimney Sweep

Chinese Puzzle

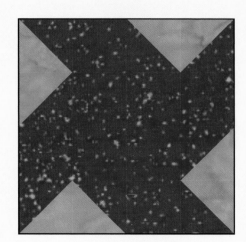

Churn Dash 1

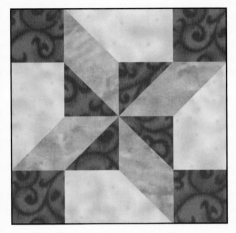

Clay's Choice

Coffin Star

Cotton Reel

Coxcomb

Crazy Ann 1

Crazy Loon

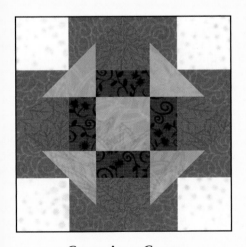

Cross in a Cross

Crosses and Losses

Crown and Star

Cube Lattice

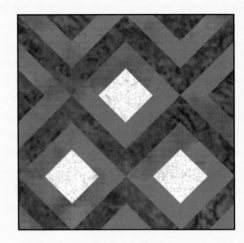

Delectable Mountains

Depression

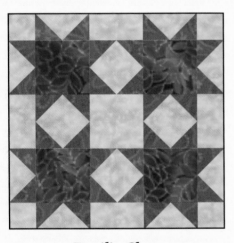

Devil's Claw

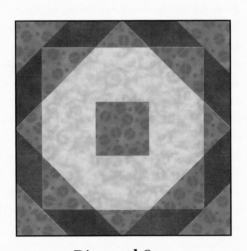

Diamond Star

Disc

Double Square

Double T

Double X

Dutchman's Puzzle

Eight Hands Around

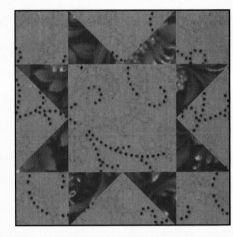

Eight-Point Star

Electric Fan

End of the Day

Eternal Triangles

Fair and Square

Fancy Stripe

Flock of Geese

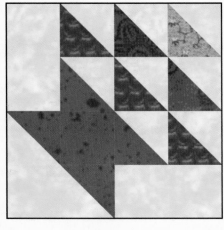

Flower Basket 1

Flyfoot

Flying Dutchman

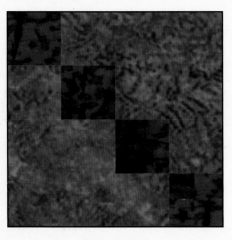

Four Patch

Fourth of July

Fox and Geese

Free Trade

Friday the 13th

Friendship

10

Georgetown Circle

Granny's Choice

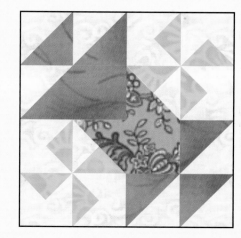

Hither and Yon

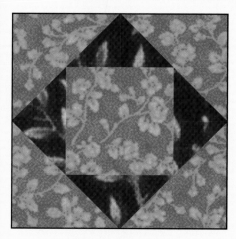

Hour Glass 1

Hour Glass 2

House that Jack Built

Hovering Birds

Indian Puzzle

Indian Star

Interwoven Puzzle

Iris

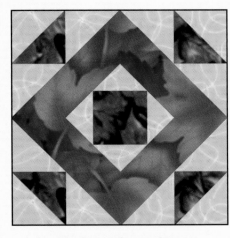

Jack in the Pulpit

Jacob's Ladder

Jewel Box

Johnnie Around the Corner

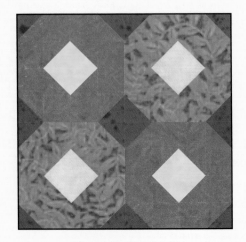

Kansas Dugout

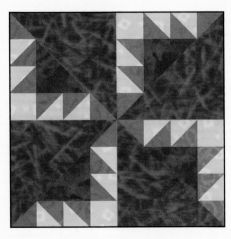

Kansas Troubles

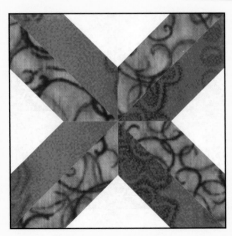

King's Cross

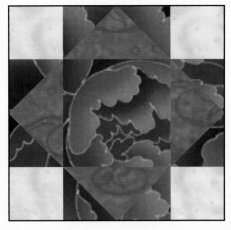

King's Crown 1

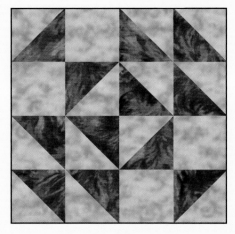

Ladies Wreath

Laurel Leaf

Lily

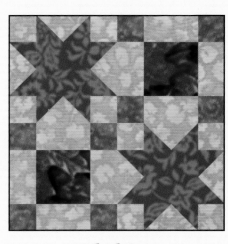

Linked Stars

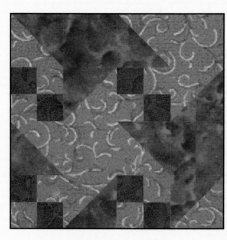

Milky Way 1

Mosaic

Mother's Choice

Mother's Dream

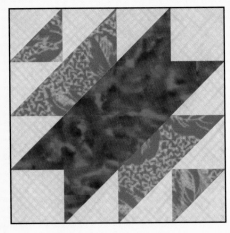

Mrs. Taft's Choice

Necktie

Next Door Neighbor

Noon and Light

Northern Lights

Ocean Waves 1

Octagon

Oh, Susannah

Old Maid's Puzzle

Old Maid's Ramble

Patience Corner

Peace and Plenty

Pinwheel Askew

Pinwheel

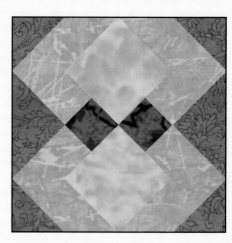

Rail Fence

Railroad Crossing

Return of the Swallows

Ribbons

15

Right and Left

Road to Oklahoma

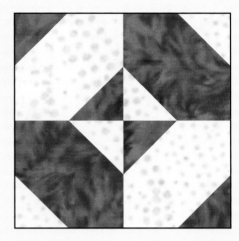

Robbing Peter to Pay Paul

Sailboat

Seesaw

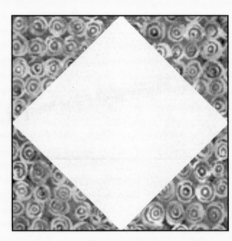

Shoofly

Shooting Square

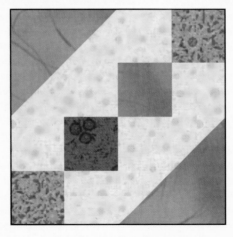

Single Irish Chain 1

Southern Belle

Square and Star

Starry Path

Stepping Stones

Streak of Lightning

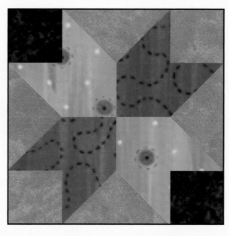

Sunlight and Shadow

Sunny Lanes

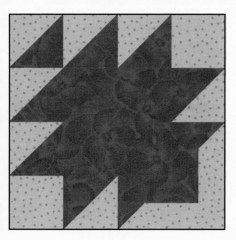

Swallows

Tea Leaf

Tippecanoe and Tyler Too

Toad in the Puddle

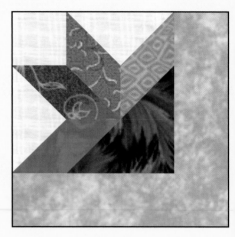

Triangles and Squares

Tulip 1

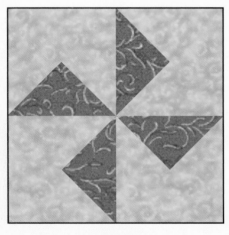

Turnstile

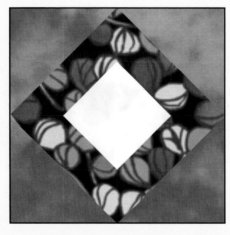

Twelve Triangles

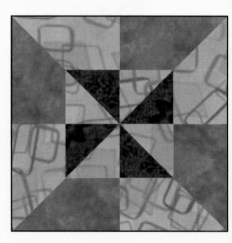

Twilight

Whirlpool

Whirlwind

White House Steps

Wild Geese

Wild Goose Chase

Wild Waves

Windblown Square

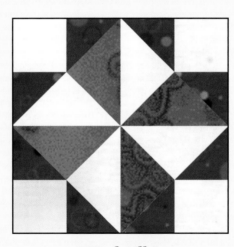

Windmill 1

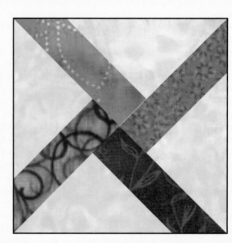

Windmill 2

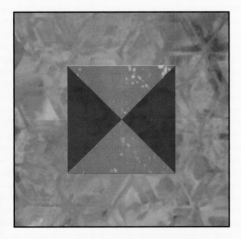

Windows

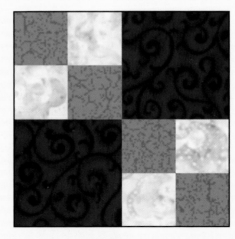

World's Fair

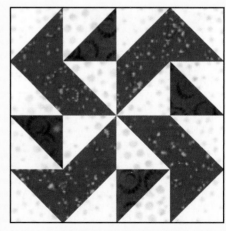

Yankee Puzzle

Five-Patch Blocks

Album 1

Album 2

Alpine Cross

Altar Light

Autumn Leaves

Baby Basket

Basket of Oranges

Basket on Point

Basket

Beginner's Delight

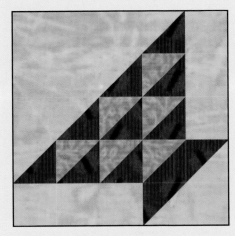

Berry Basket

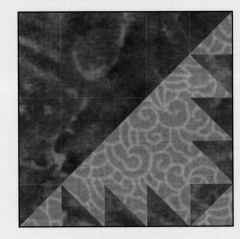

Big Basket

Broken Arrows 1

Broken Arrows 2

Broken Irish Chain

Butterfly at the Crossroads

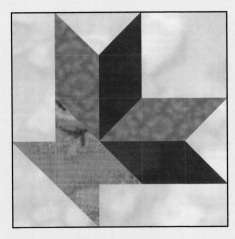

Cactus Basket 2

Cain and Abel

Cake Stand

Captain's Wheel

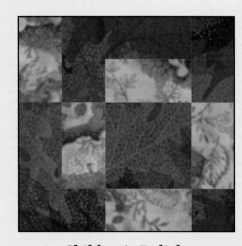

Children's Delight

Christmas Tree 1

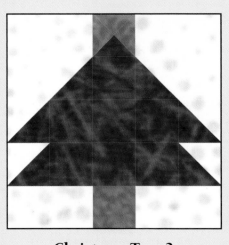

Christmas Tree 2

Churn Dash 2

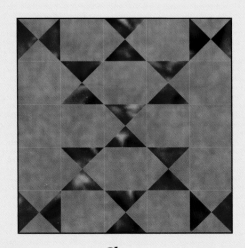

Clown

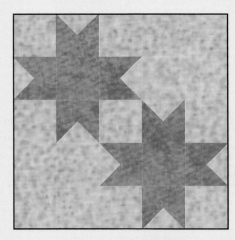

Cluster of Stars

Cobblestones

Corn and Beans

Courthouse Steps

Crazy Ann 2

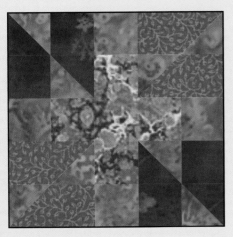

Crazy House

Criss Cross

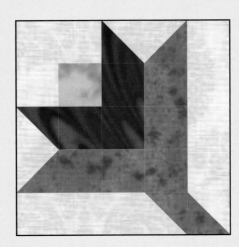

Crocus

Cross and Crown

Cross Patch

Crossroads

Domino Star

Domino

Double Duty

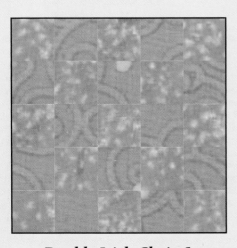

Double Irish Chain 1

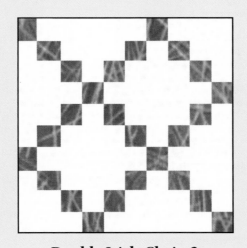

Double Irish Chain 2

Double Irish Chain 3

Double Irish Chain 4

Double V

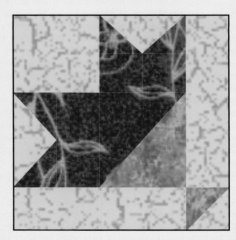

Dove at the Window

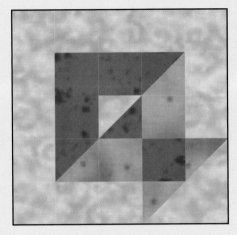

Dresden Basket

Duck and Ducklings

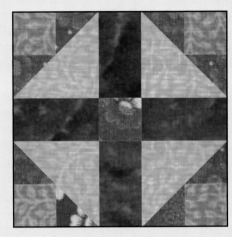

Duck's Foot

Eagle

Eve's Garden

Farmer's Daughter

Fish

Flower Basket 2

Flower Pot 1

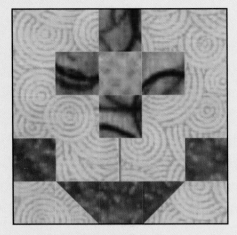

Flower Pot 2

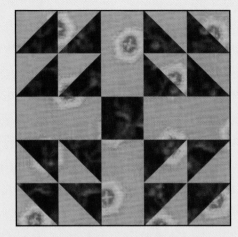

Flying Geese 1

Flying Geese 2

Flying Stars

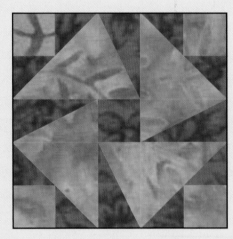

Follow the Leader

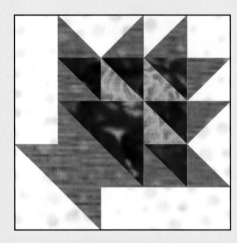

Fruit Basket

Gamecocks

Garden of Eden

Gold Brick

Golden Crowns

Goose Tracks

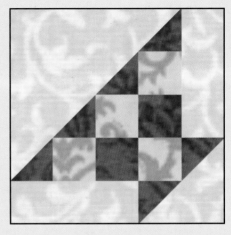

Grandmother's Basket

Grandmother's Choice

Grandmother's Puzzle

Greek Cross

Guam

Halley's Comet

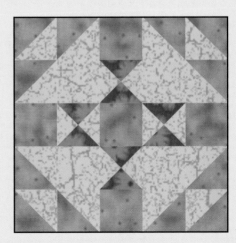

Handy Andy

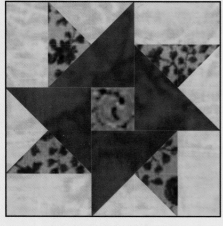

Hope of Hartford

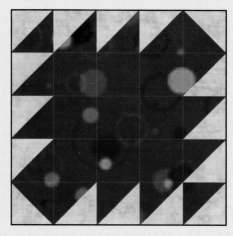

Indian Block

Indian Trail

Jack in the Box

Jack's Block

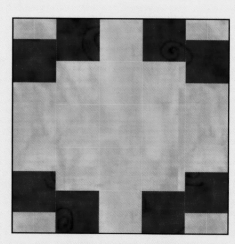

Jericho Walls

Job's Troubles

King's Crown 2

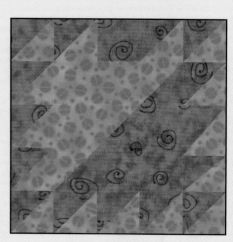

Lady of the Lake

28

Lincoln Block

Lone Cross

Maine

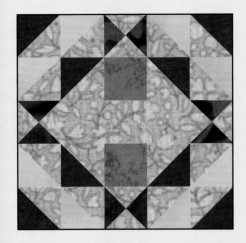

Memory

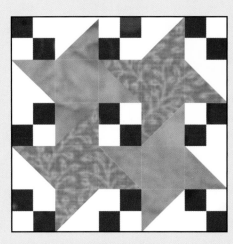

Milky Way 2

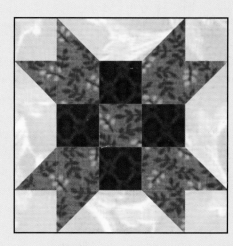

Miller's Daughter

Monkey Wrench

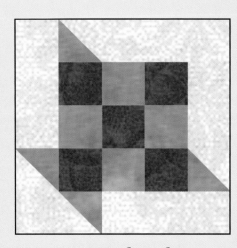

Nine Patch Basket

Nine Patch Star

Norway Pine Tree

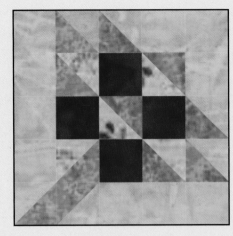

Nosegay

Ocean Waves 2

Odd Scraps

Old Italian

Ozark Trail

Patch Blossom

Patchwork Scraps

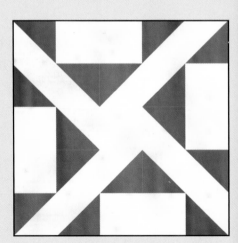

Pathfinder

Philadelphia

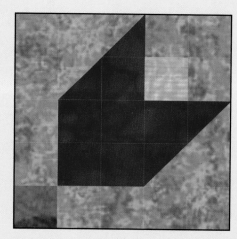

Pieced Tulip

Pine Tree

Pinwheel Square

Prized Possession

Providence

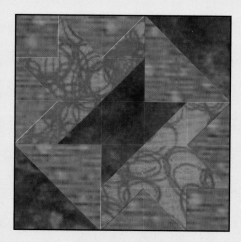

Queen's Crown

Red Cross

Rocky Mountain Chain

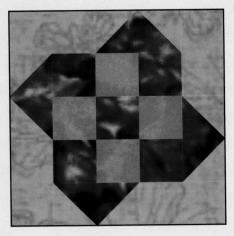

Rolling Five Patch

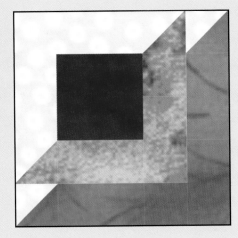

Rosebud 1

Rosebud 2

Round the Corner

Sawtooth 1

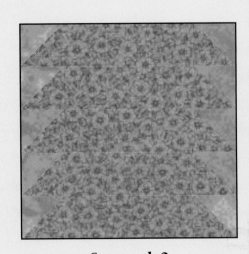

Sawtooth 2

Simple Design

Single Chain and Knot

Single Irish Chain 2

Single Wedding Ring

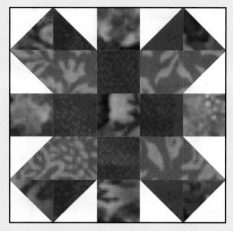

Sister's Choice

Southern Pine

Southwest Cross

Souvenir

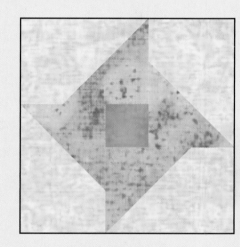

Spinning Star

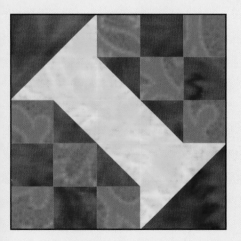

Spool of Thread

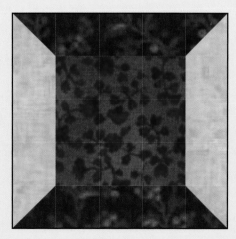

Spool

Square and Half Square

Square and Squares

St. Louis Star

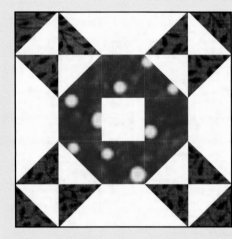

Star and Octagon

Steps to the Altar

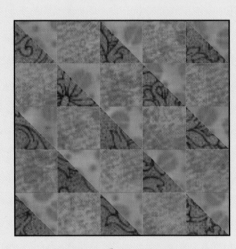

Strength in Union

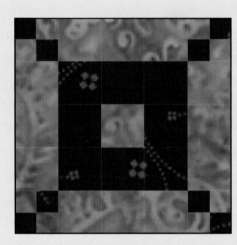

Sunbeam

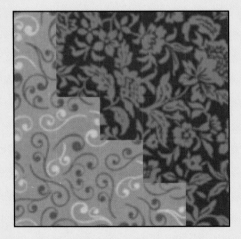

Sunshine and Shadow

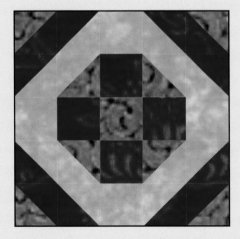

Target

Tulip 2

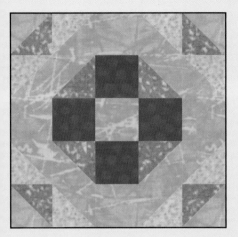

Wedding Ring 1

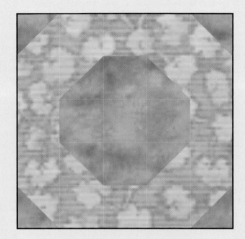

Wedding Ring 2

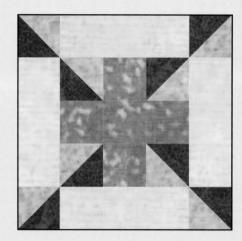

Whirling Square

Wild Goose Chase Five Patch

Wind Wheel

Windows and Doors

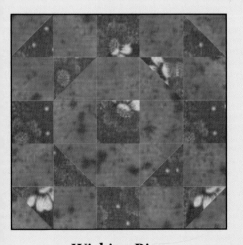

Wishing Ring

Woven Five Patch

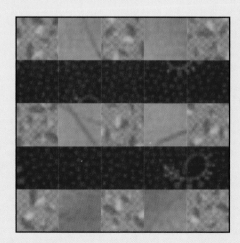

Woven Ribbons

Star Blocks: Four Patch

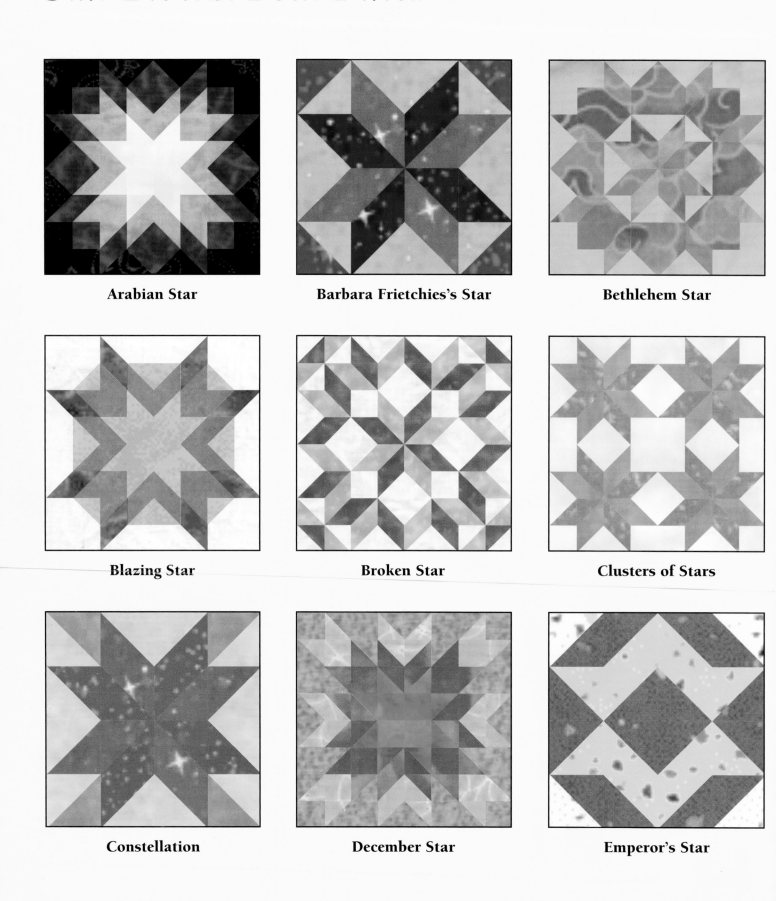

Arabian Star

Barbara Frietchies's Star

Bethlehem Star

Blazing Star

Broken Star

Clusters of Stars

Constellation

December Star

Emperor's Star

Enclosed Stars

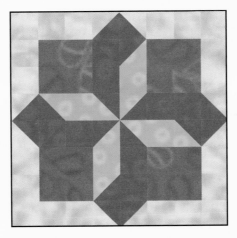

Enigma Star

Evening Star 1

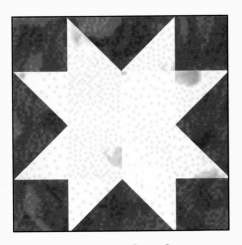

Evening Star 2

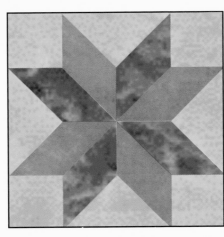

LeMoyne Star

Missouri Star

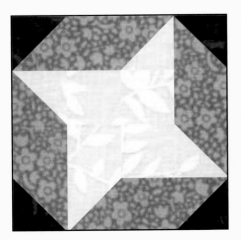

North Star

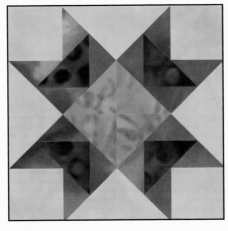

Northumberland Star

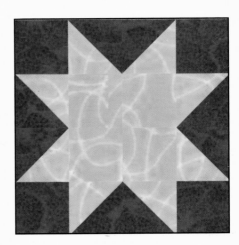

Odd Fellows Star

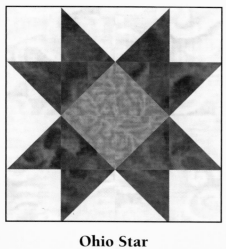

Ohio Star

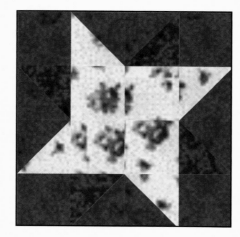

Pale Star

Patriotic Star

Pieced Star 1

Pieced Star 2

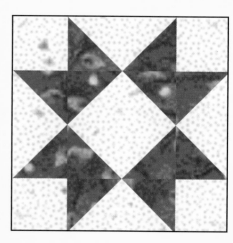

Ribbon Star Four Patch

Ring Around the Star

Rising Star

Royal Star

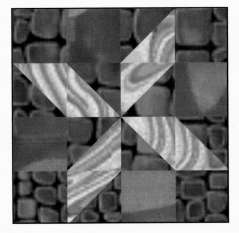

Shooting Star

Spinning Star Wheel

Star and Chains

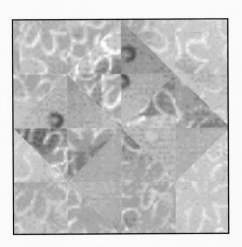

Star of Four Points

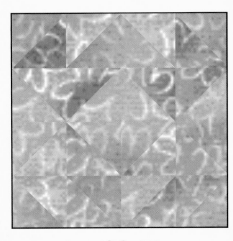

Star of the West

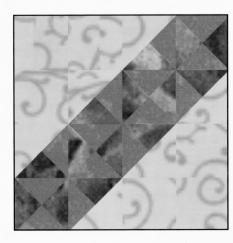

Straight Starry Path

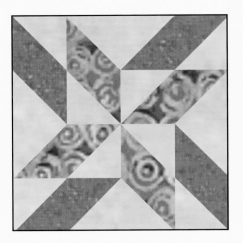

Trailing Star

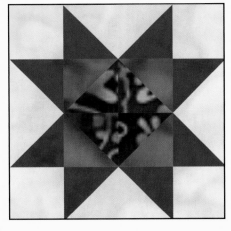

Variable Star

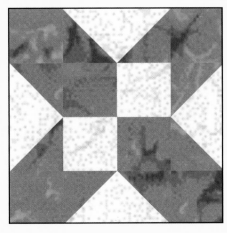

Winged Four-Patch Star

Star Blocks: Nine Patch

Amish Star

Arkansas Star

Arrowhead Star Variation

Arrowhead Star

Braced Star

Bright Star

Christmas Star

Combination Star

Crossed Paths Star

Danish Star

Diamond Star 1

Diamond Star 2

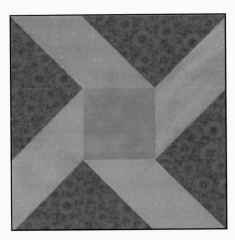

Eccentric Star 1

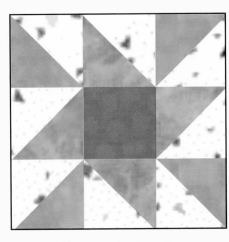

Eccentric Star 2

Eccentric Star 3

Eight-Pointed Star 1

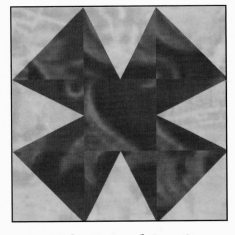

Eight-Pointed Star 2

Evening Star

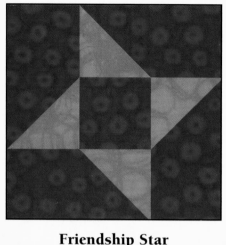

Friendship Star

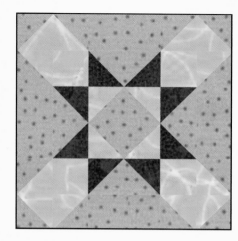

Lone Star

Maltese Star

May Star

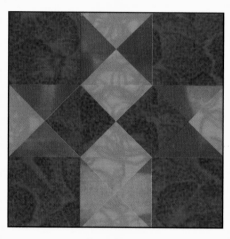

Midnight Star

Ornate Star

Pinwheel Star 1

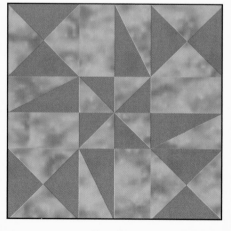

Pinwheel Star 2

Ribbon Star Nine Patch

Shining Star in the Sky

Silent Star

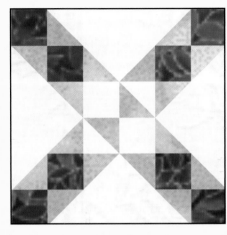

Star Explosion

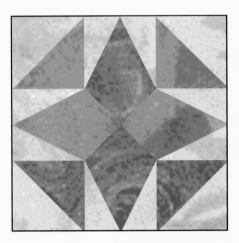

Star of the Sea

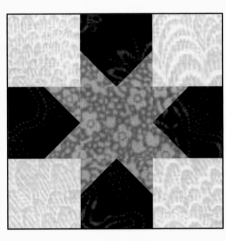

Star of Wonder

Starry Sky

Twin Star

Union Star

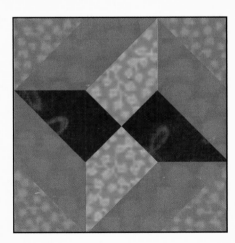

Wandering Star

Nine Patch Blocks

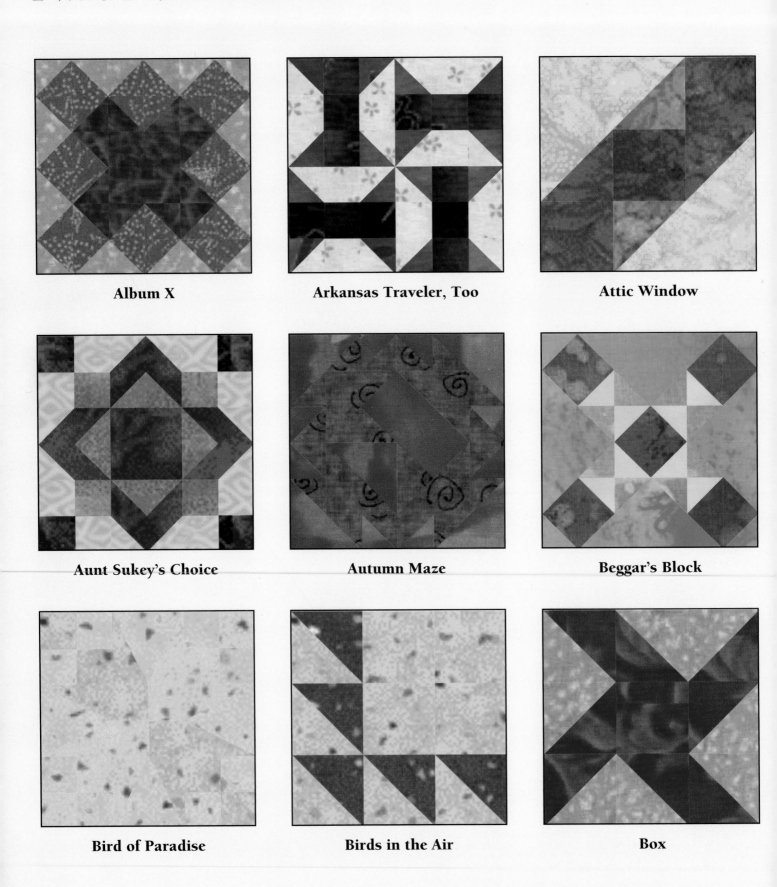

Album X

Arkansas Traveler, Too

Attic Window

Aunt Sukey's Choice

Autumn Maze

Beggar's Block

Bird of Paradise

Birds in the Air

Box

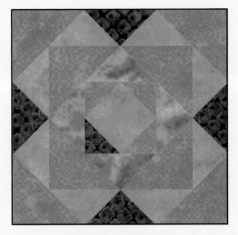

Boxes on Boxes

Bridal Bouquet

Builder's Blocks

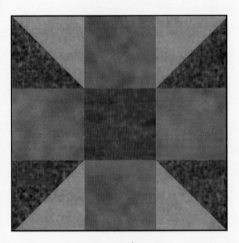

Calico Puzzle

Carnival Time

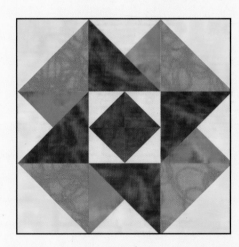

Castle

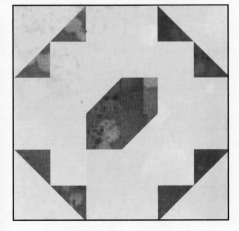

Cedars of Lebanon

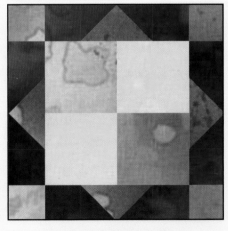

Chained Nine Patch

Chinese Quilt Block

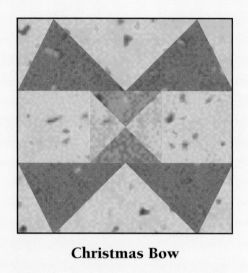

Christmas Bow

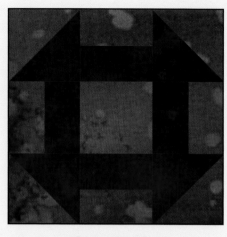

Churn Dash 3

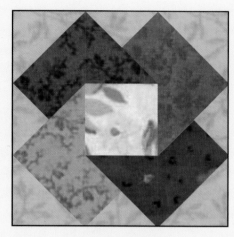

Color Wheel

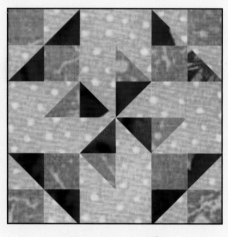

Contrary Wife

Corn and Beans Nine Patch

Cross

Crosses and Losses 2

Cut Glass Dish

Cut the Corners

Dancing Pinwheels

Dandy

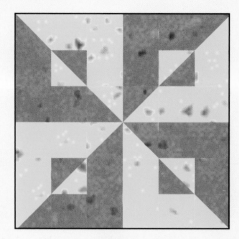

Delight

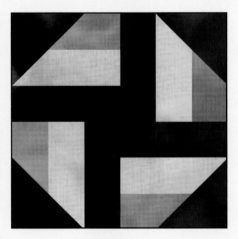

Double L

Double Pyramid

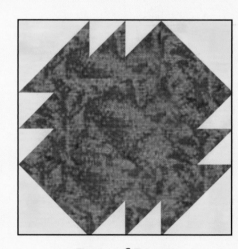

Dove of Peace

Dublin Steps

Dumbell

Empty Spool

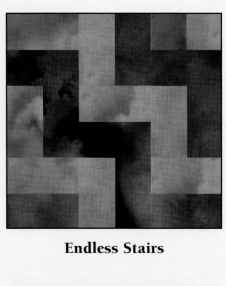

Endless Stairs

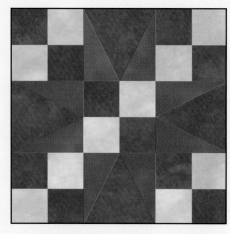

Fifty-four Forty or Fight

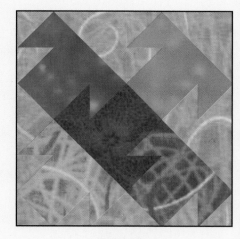

Five T's

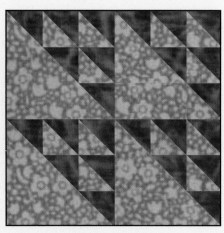

Flocks of Geese

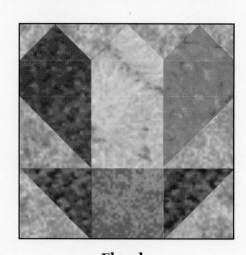

Florals

Flutter Wheel

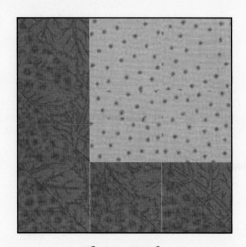

Flying Birds

Flying Dutchman Zig Zag

Flying Shuttles

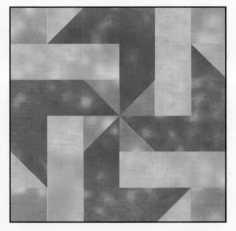

Follow the Leader Around

Four Corners

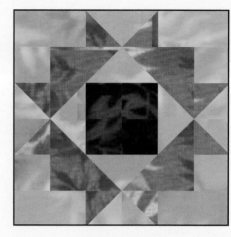

Four Crowns

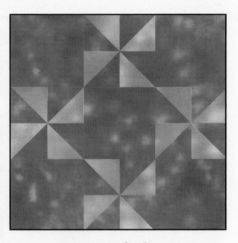

Four Leaf Clover

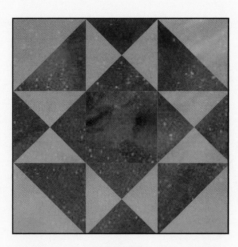

Four X's

Foxes and Geese

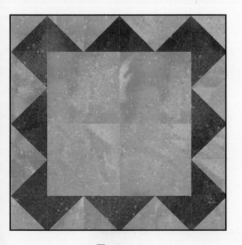

Frame

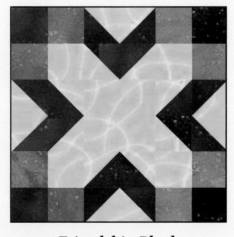

Friendship Block

Fringed Square

Garden Path

Gentleman's Fancy

Golden Stairs

Greek Cross in a Square

Halloween

Handy Dandy

Happy Home

Hay's Corner

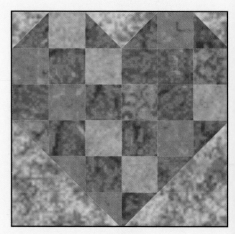

Heart

Hill and Valley

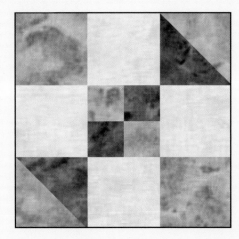

Hour Glass

Housewife

Hovering Hawks

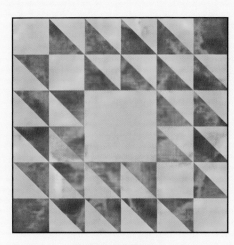

Indian Plume

Indian Puzzle Piece

Interlocked Squares

Jack's Delight

Jacob's Ladder Nine Patch

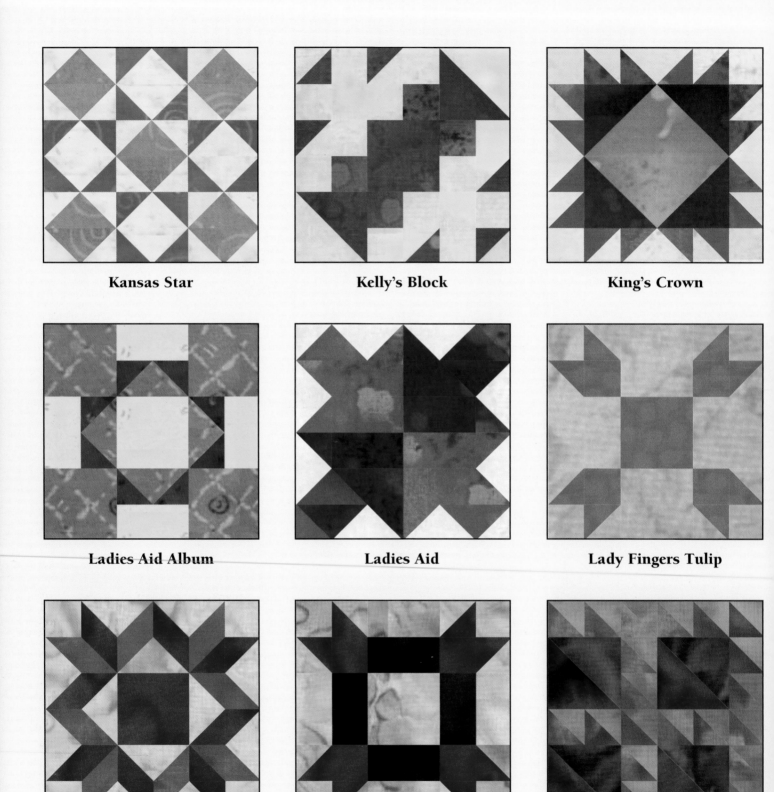

Kansas Star	**Kelly's Block**	**King's Crown**
Ladies Aid Album	**Ladies Aid**	**Lady Fingers Tulip**
Laurel Wreath	**Linoleum**	**Lost Ships**

Lover's Lane

Many T's

Maple Leaf

Mayflower

Memory Game

Merry Kite

Monkey Wrench Tool

Morning

Mosaic Tile

Mrs. Bryan's Choice

Mrs. Morgan's Choice

Mystery Block

Neckties

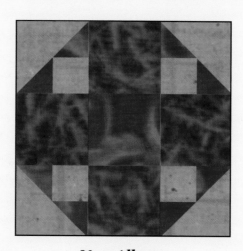

New Album

1941 Nine Patch

Nonsense

Noon and Night

Northwind

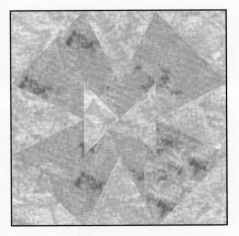

Old Grey Goose

Old Tippecanoe

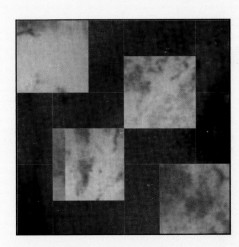

Optical Illusion

Ozark Maple Leaf

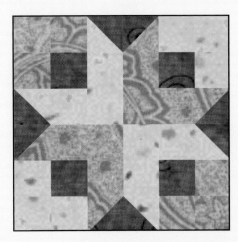

Pandora's Box

Patience Corners

Picket Fence

Pinwheel Double

Practical Orchard

Prairie Flower

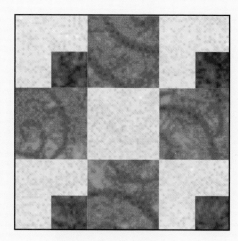

Puss in the Corner

Right Hand of Friendship

Road to the White House

Robbing Peter

Rocky Road to California

Rolling Pinwheel

Rolling Stone

Roman Square

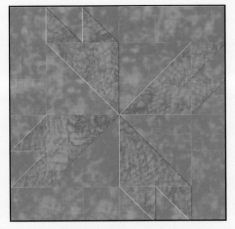

Rosebuds Twirling

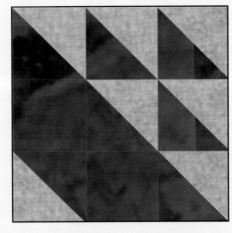

Sailboat on an Angle

Sailing Schooner

Scrap Basket

Shaded Trail

Shadow Box

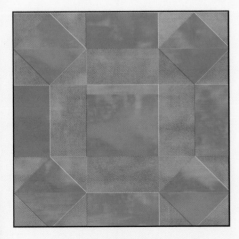

Single Wedding Band

Snowball

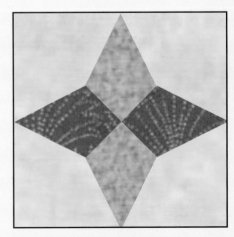

Snowflake

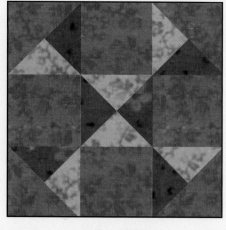

Spider Webs

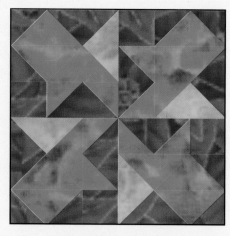

Spinning Wheel

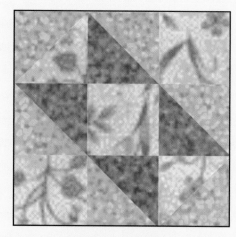

Split Nine Patch

Squirrel in a Cage

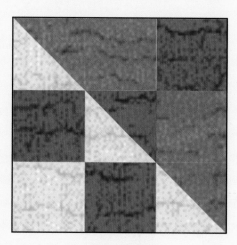

Straight Furrow

Straw Flowers

Strawberry Basket

Swamp Patch

Swing in the Center

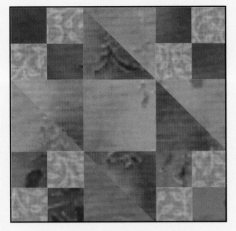

Tail of Benjamin's Kite

Tangled Briars

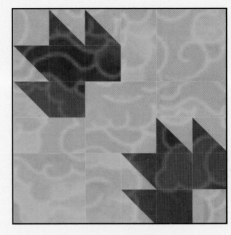

Tea Leaves

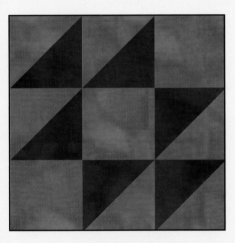

Tennessee

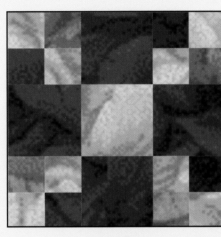

Thrifty

Tic Tac Toe

Treasure Box

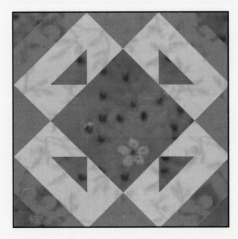

Treasure Chest

Tree of Paradise

Triangles

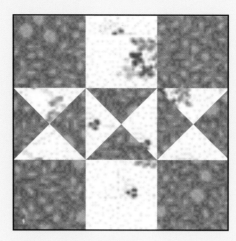

Triplet

True Blue

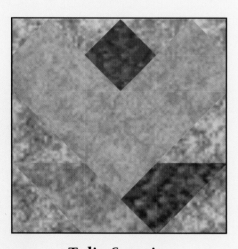

Tulip Surprise

Tulip on an Angle

Turkey in the Straw

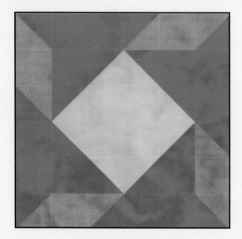

Turkish Puzzle

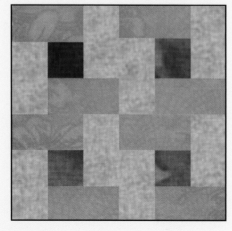

Twists

Union

Water Wheel

Weathervane

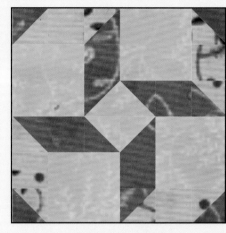

Whirlaround

Whirling Whirlpool

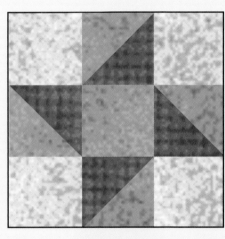

Windmill

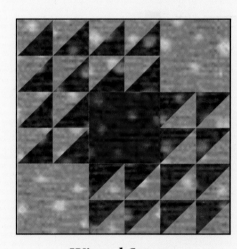

Winged Square

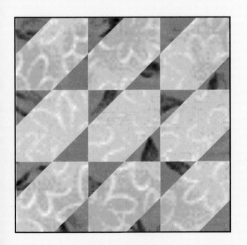

X-quisite

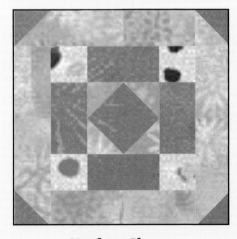

Yankee Charm

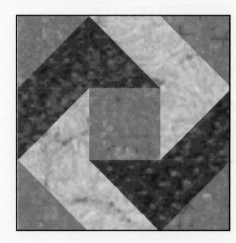

Zig Zag Path

Curved Blocks

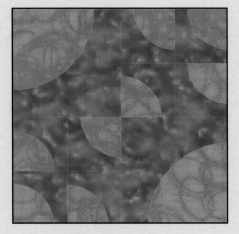

Birds in the Corners

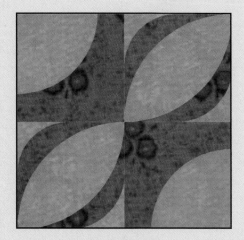

Bow

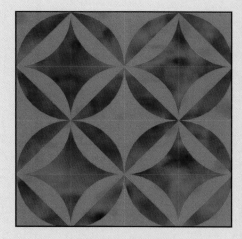

Broken Plates

Broken Flower

Butterfly Flower

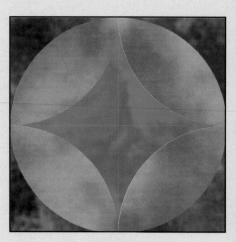

Circle and Star

Circles and Curves

Circles and Squares

Circles in Circles

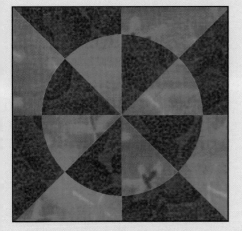

Circular Pinwheel

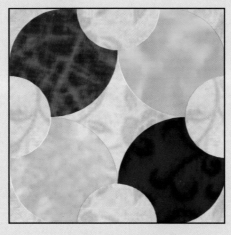

Colorful Shells

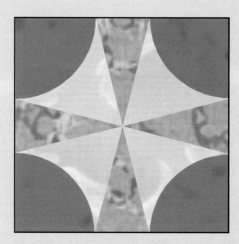

Curtain Call

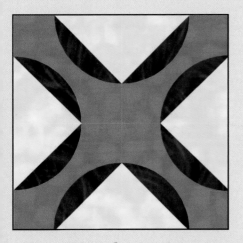

Curved Arrows

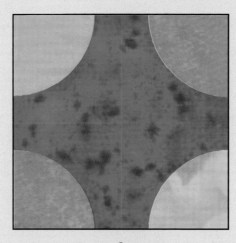

Curved Cross

Curved Posy

Curved Zig Zag

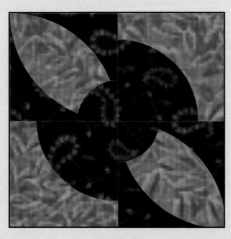

Curvy

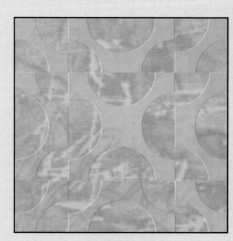

Dog Bones

Drunkard's Trails

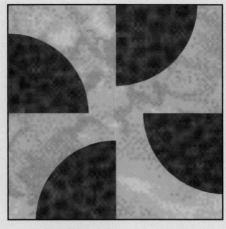

Drunkard's Pinwheel

Fancy Circle Fan

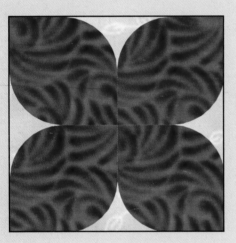

Fat Petals

Flower in the Middle

Flowers and Stems

Four Petals

Framed Petals

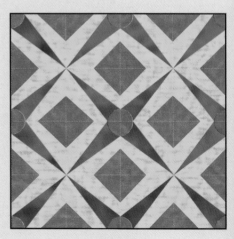

Geometric

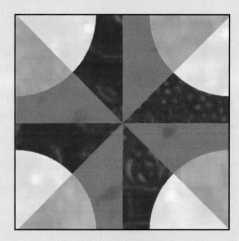

Highlighted Posy

Hugs and Kisses

Light and Dark

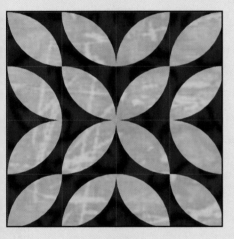

Lots of Leaves

Melon Around the World

Mixed Petals

Nuts and Bolts

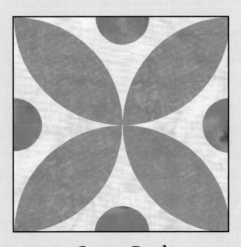

Orange Petal

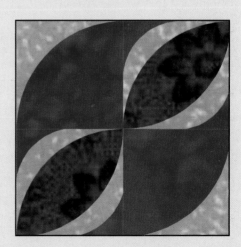

Ovals in Ovals

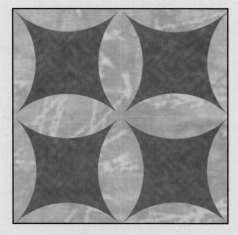

Overlapping Circles

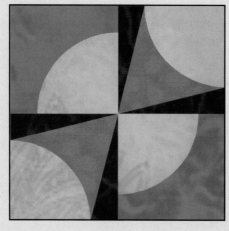

Pair of Megaphones

Parading Pinwheels

Pastel Petals

Pearls

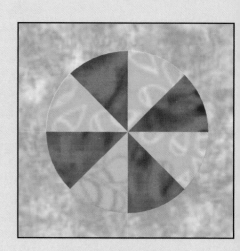

Peppermint Candy

Petal Power

Petal Tile

Petals and Dots

Petals on Point

Pie and Pinwheel

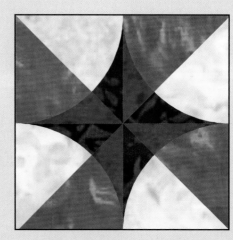

Pinwheel Curved Star

Pinwheel Tile

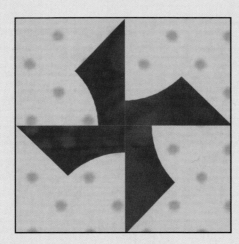

Plain Fancy

Pointy Star

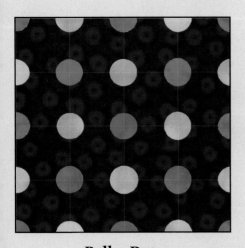

Polka Dots

Propellar

Rays of Hope

Scallops

Seaweed

Shouts of Joy

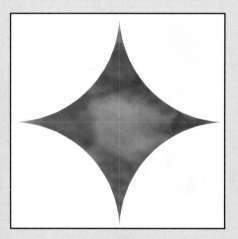

Simplicity

Solar Eclipse

Southwest Curves

Subtle Petals

Summer Fan

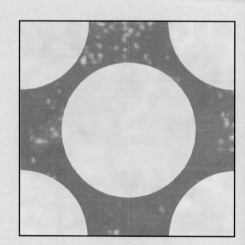

Sunshine

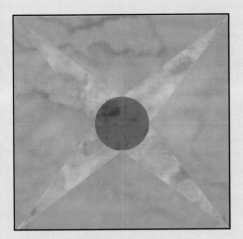

To the Point

Trip Around the World

Tropical Petals

Trumpets

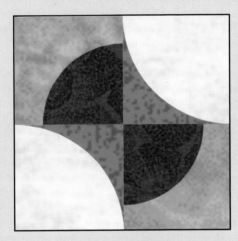

Unfinished Bow

Waves

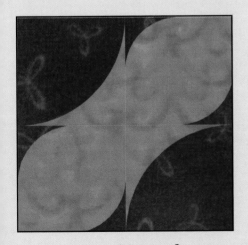

Wavy Diagonal

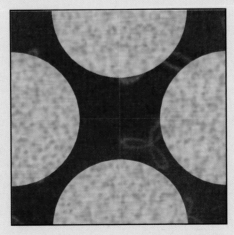

X Marks the Spot

Zig Zag Petals

Foundation Blocks: Pictures

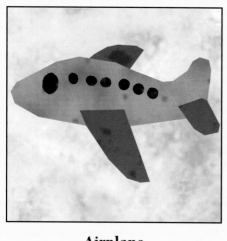

Airplane

Angel in Springtime

Angel Prayer

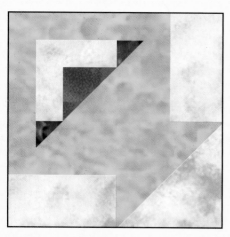

Apple basket

Baby Angel

Basic House

Bee

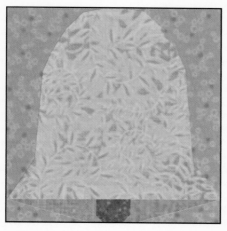

Bell

Bird 1

Bird 2

Black Crow

Blue Bells

Blue Bird

Brown Bird

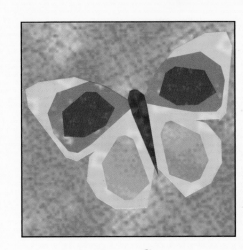

Butterfly

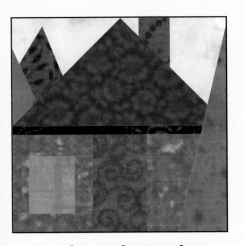

Cabin in the Woods

Cat

Cherry

Colorful Butterfly

Country Cottage

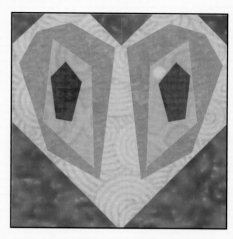

Crazy Heart

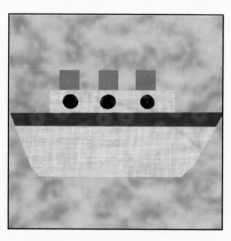

Cruise Ship

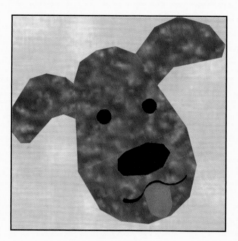

Dog 1

Dog 2

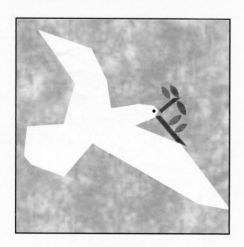

Dove

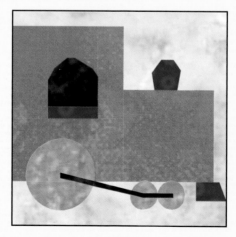

Engine

Film Strip

Finch

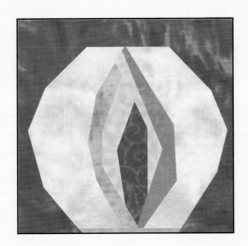

Fire

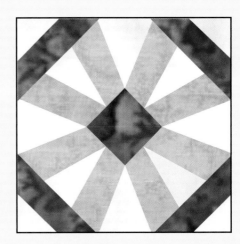

Flat Bow

Floating Airship

Flowing Angel

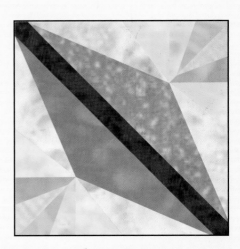

Flying Saucer

Frog

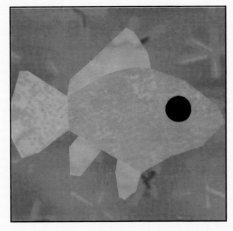

Gold Fish

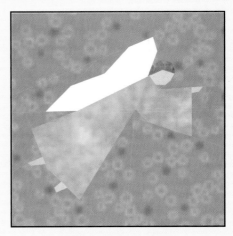

Heavenly Angel

Helicopter

Hot Air Balloon

House with an Attic

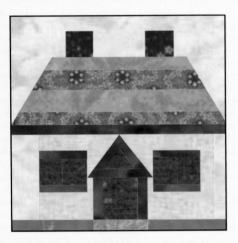

House

Jet

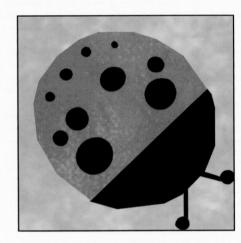

Lady Bug

Lighthouse

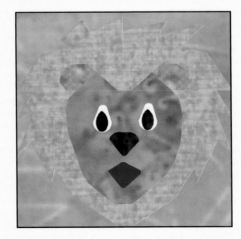

Lion

Little Lamb

Lovely Angel

Lovely Home

Monkey

Mountain Lake

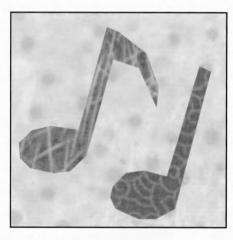

Music Notes

Music

Musical Notes

Oveall Sam Formal

Overall Sam

Peaceful Angel

Pedestal Basket

Present

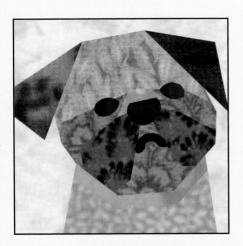

Pug Portrait

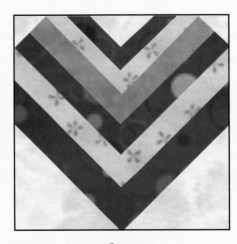

Purple Heart

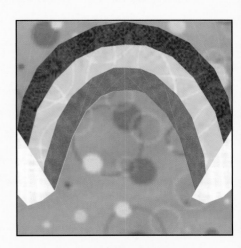

Rainbow

Ribbons 2

Sailing Sailboat

Sailing

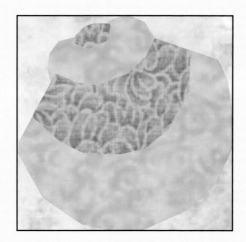

Seahorse

Seashell

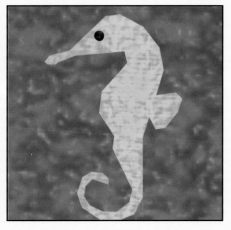

Simple Basket

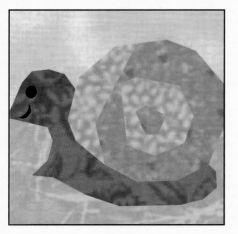

Snail

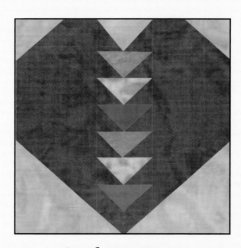

Southwest Heart

Squares and Diamonds

Striped Heart

Sunbonnet Sue Formal

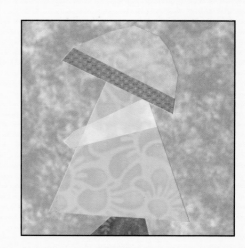

Sunbonnet Sue

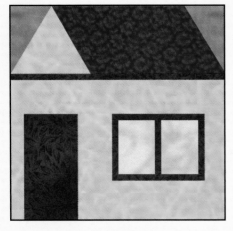

Sunny House

Teddy Bear

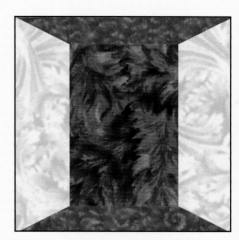

Thread Spool

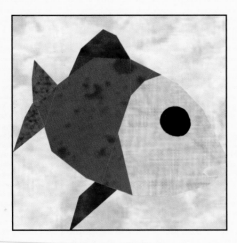

Tropical Fish

Truck

Trucking

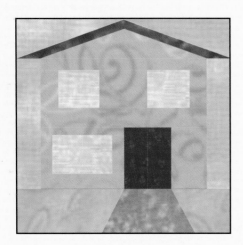

Two Story House

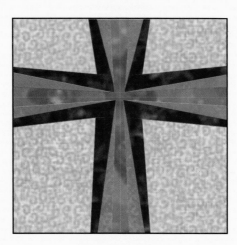

Upright Cross

Winter Cabin

Foundation Blocks: Flowers, Trees, Fruit and Veggies

Abstract Flower

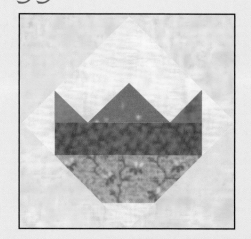

Angled Bud

Apple

Banana

Budding Flower

Buds in the Corners

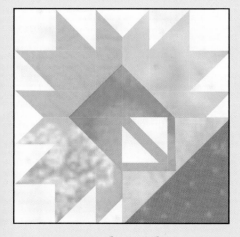

Carolina Lily

Carrot

Closed Tulip

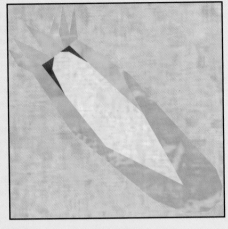

Corn

Daisy

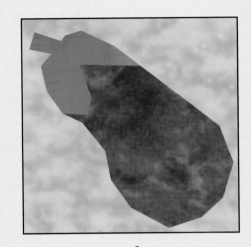

Eggplant

Elegant Rose Bud

Floral Bud

Flower Bowl

Flower Fan

Flower

Fruit Tree

Full Basket

Green Leaf

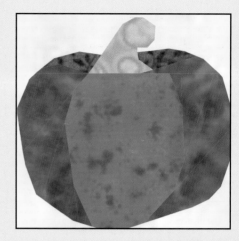

Green Pepper

Heart Flowers

Leaf

Lemon

Log Cabin Rose

Mum

Palm Branch

Palm Tree in the Wind

Palm Tree

Pear

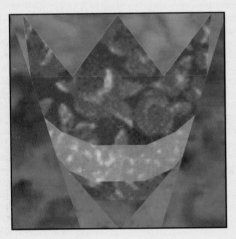

Perky Tulip

Pine Tree

Pineapple

Pot of Flowers

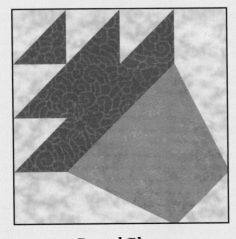

Potted Plant

Pretty Flower

Rose Bud

Rose

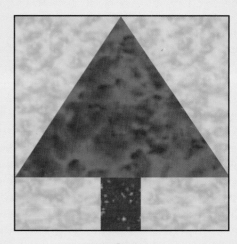

Simple Tree

Single Tulip

Strawberry

Summer Flower

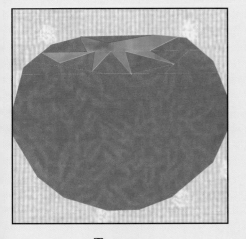

Tomato

Tree in Winter

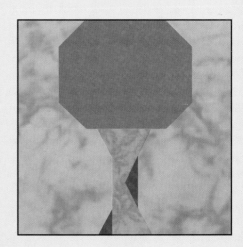

Tree

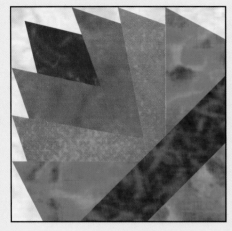

Tulip Bud

Tulip Foursome

Tulip in a Basket

Tulip Patch

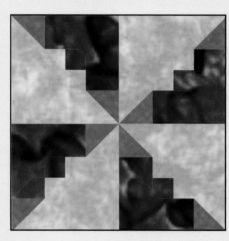

Tulip Pinwheel

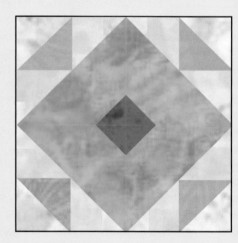

Tulips in the Corners

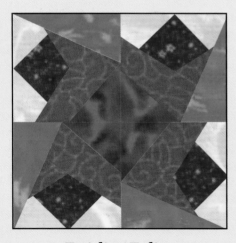

Twirling Tulips

Water Lily

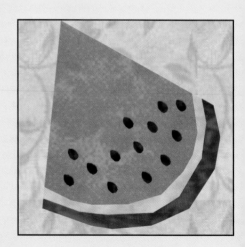

Watermelon

Foundation Blocks: Stars and Pinwheels

Abstract Star

Block Pinwheel

Cabin Star

Chubby Star

Colorful Eight-Point Star

Colorful Stars

Curved Pinwheel

Double Star

Exquisite Star

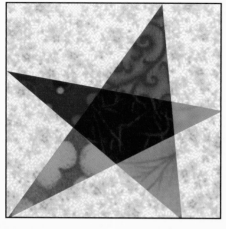

Falling Star

Fancy Star

Five-Pointed Star

Five Point Star

Flaming Wheel

Fractured Pinwheel

Framed Star

Frisbee Star

Hidden Pinwheel

Hidden Star

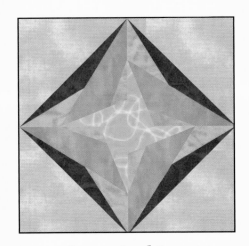

Intertwined Star

Intricate Star

Leaning Star

Mosaic Star

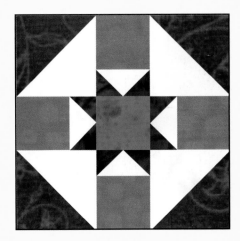

Patchwork Star

Patchwork

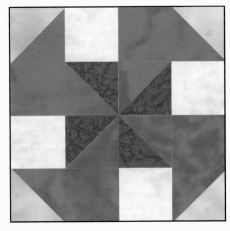

Pinwheel Baby Block

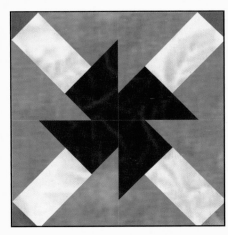

Pinwheel Crossing

Pinwheel Flower

Pinwheel in a Star

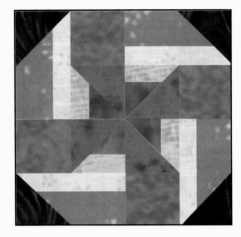

Pinwheel Parade

Propeller Pinwheel

Rolling Star

Round Pinwheel

Shining Star

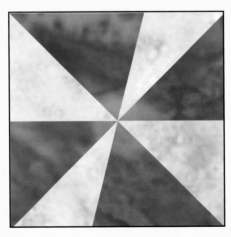

Simple Pinwheel

Simple Star

Simply Striped Pinwheel

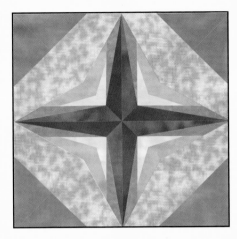

Special Star

Spiderweb Star

Spiked Pinwheel

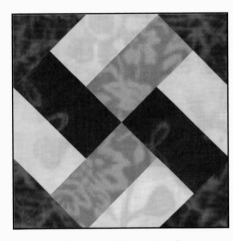

Square Pinwheel

Star Crossing

Star Echo

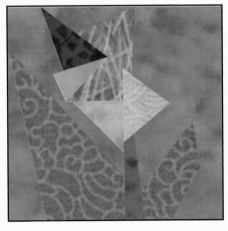

Star Flower 1

Star Flower 2

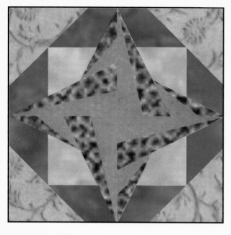

Star in a Box 1

Star in a Box 2

Star in a Pinwheel

Star in the Sky

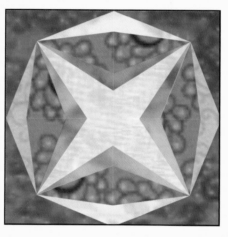

Star Jewel

Star of David 2

Star of Many Colors

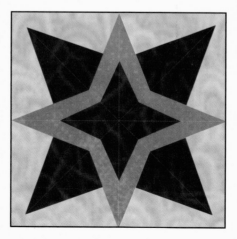

Star Power 1

Star Power 2

Star Rays

Star Swirl

Star with Pinwheel

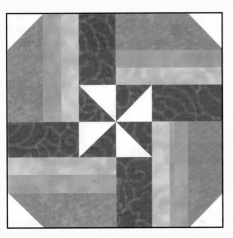

Stripes and Pinwheel

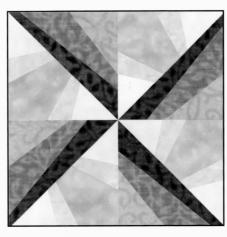

Stripes Twirling

Triple Star

Twisting Pinwheel

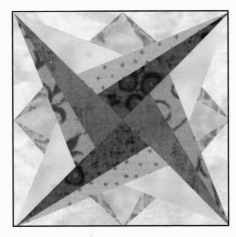

Whirling Star

Wide Star

Foundation Blocks: Holidays & Celebrations

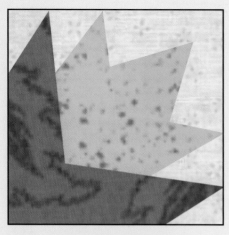

Autumn Flower

Birthday Cake

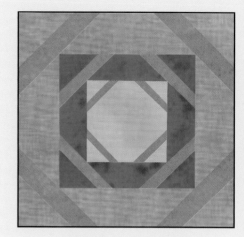

Birthday Present

Black Cat

Candy Corn

Christmas Angel

Christmas Posy

Christmas Star Snowflake

Christmas Tree

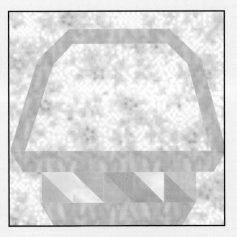

Easter Basket

Easter Bunny

Edged Valentine Heart

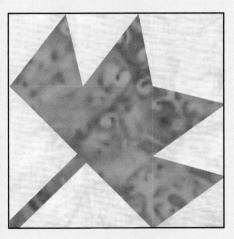

Fall Leaf 1

Fall Leaf 2

Flag

Flying Flag

Halloween Pinwheel

Halloween Pumpkin

Hexagon Snowflake

Icicle Star

Noel

Paper Snowflade

Patriotic Heart

Patriotic Starburst

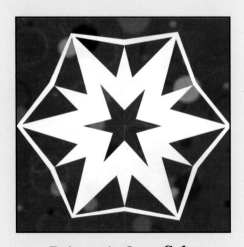

Poinsettia Snowflake

Santa

Shamrock

Snowflake Star

Snowman

Star of Bethlehem

Star of David

Turkey

Uncle Sam Hat

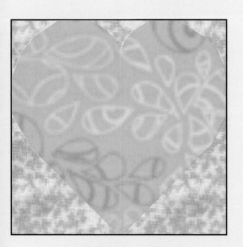

Valentine Heart

Winter Pine

Witch's Hat

Foundation Blocks: Letters and Numbers
Block Alphabet & Numbers

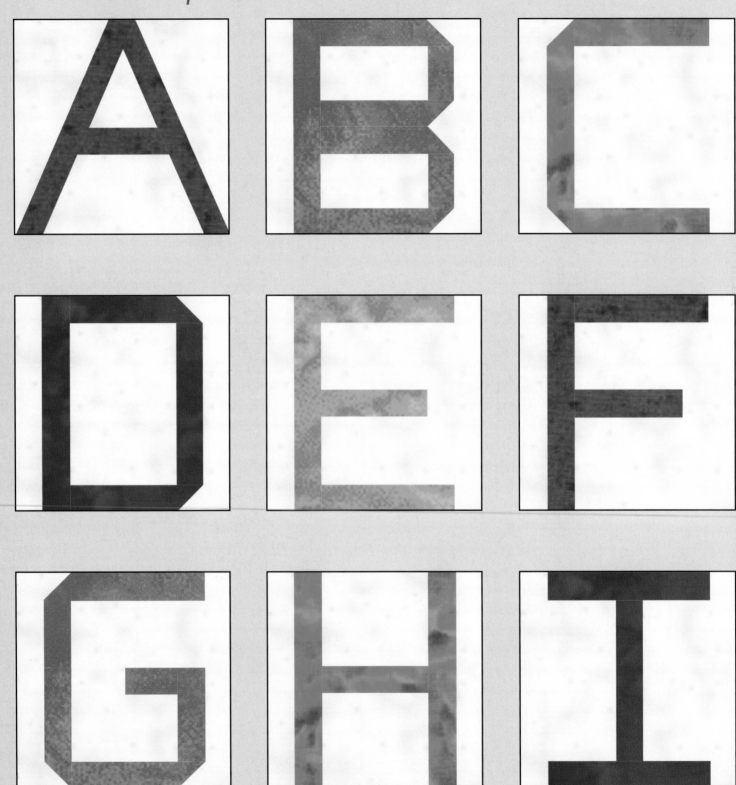

J K L

M N O

P Q R

S T U
V W X
Y Z O

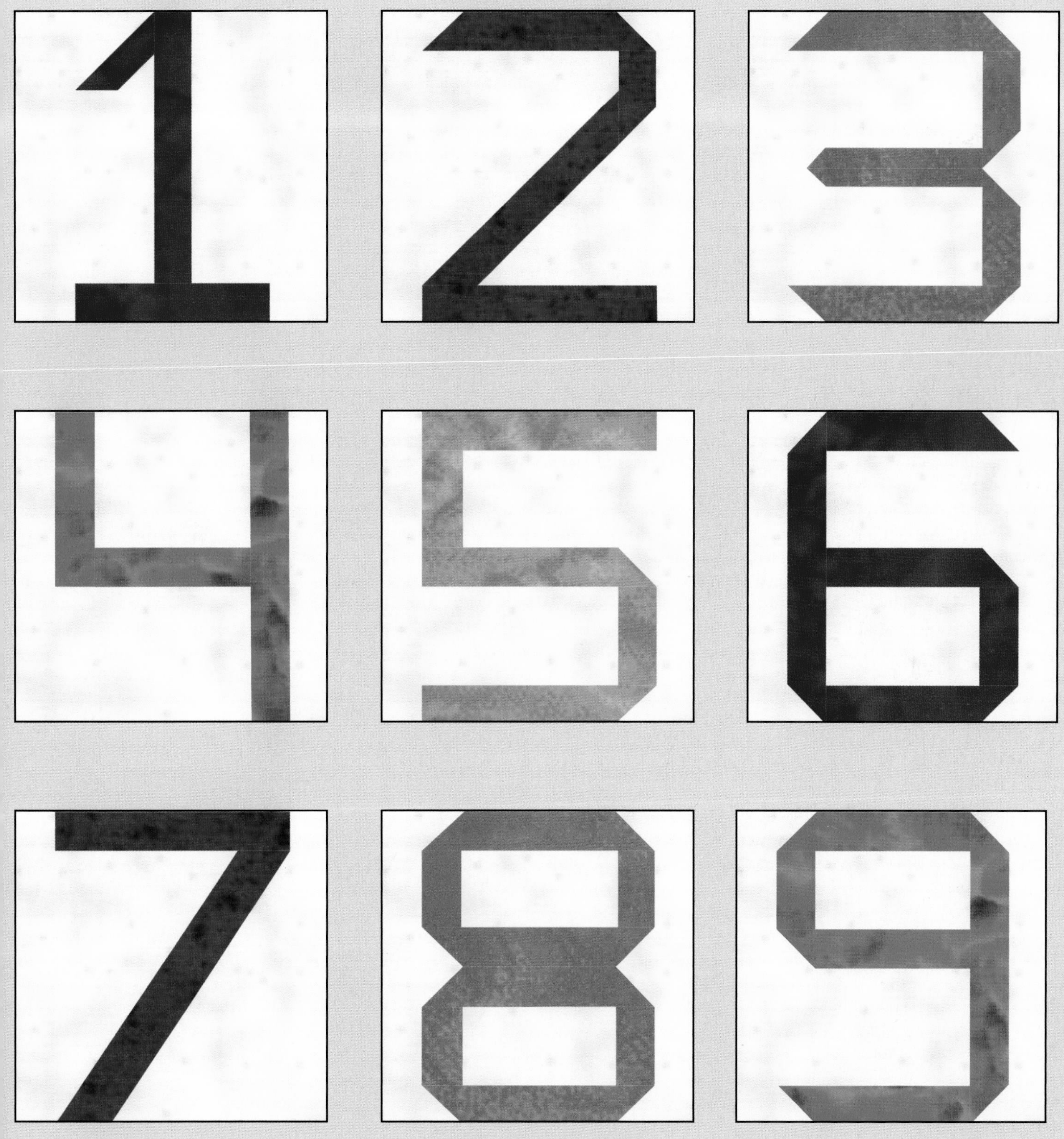

Kid's Alphabet & Numbers

 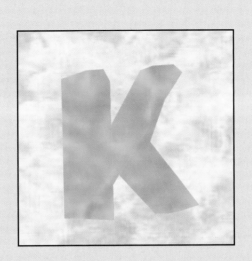 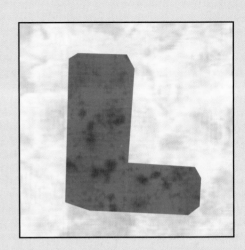

  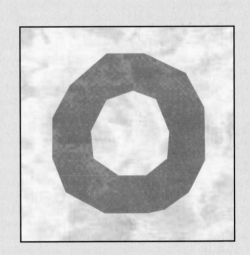

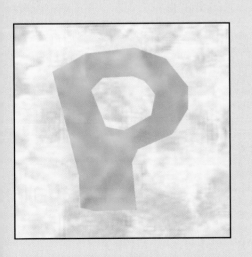 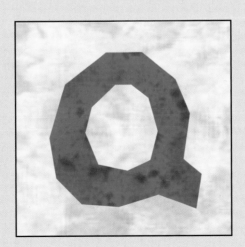 

  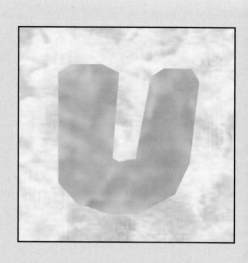

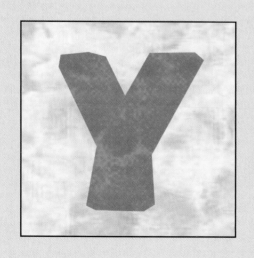 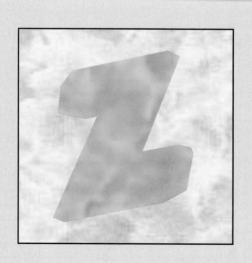 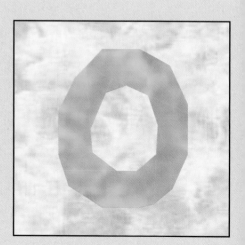

Foundation Blocks: Patchwork

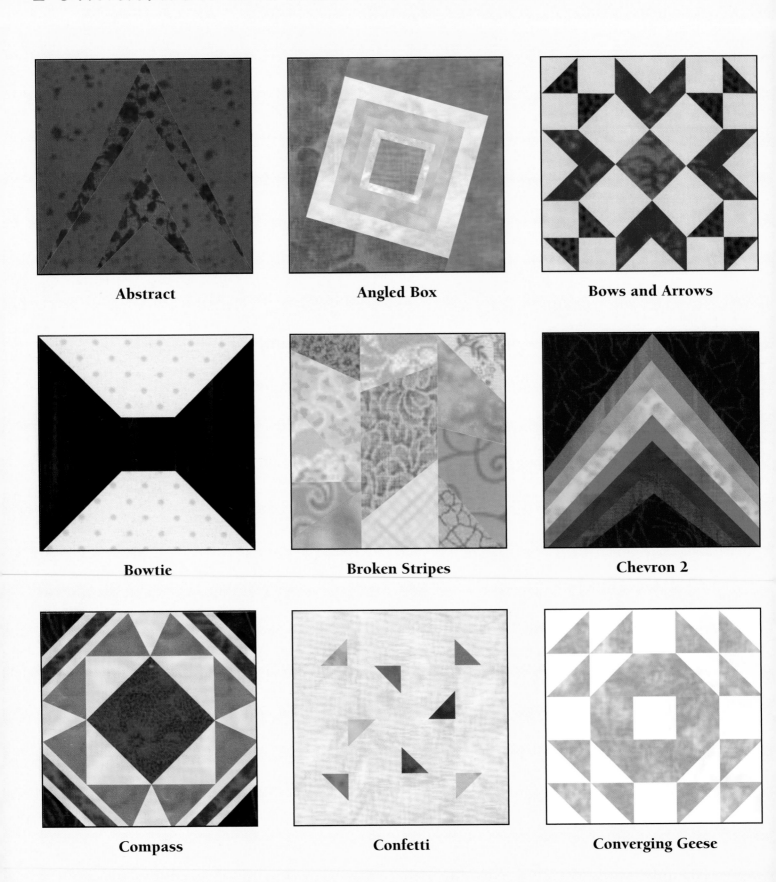

Abstract

Angled Box

Bows and Arrows

Bowtie

Broken Stripes

Chevron 2

Compass

Confetti

Converging Geese

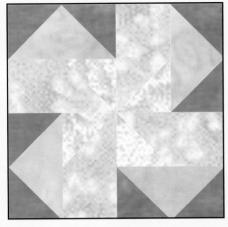

Corner Pinwheel

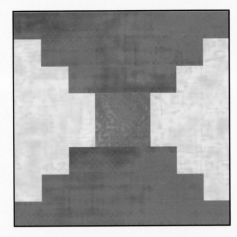

Courthouse Steps 2

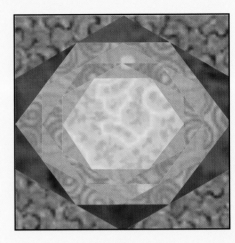

Crazy Hexagon

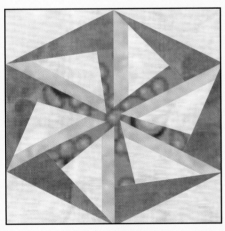

Crazy Wheel

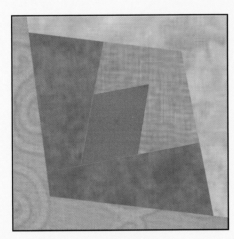

Crooked Logs

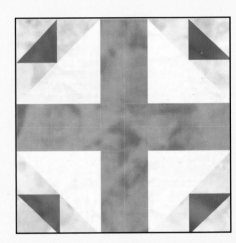

Cross and Triangles

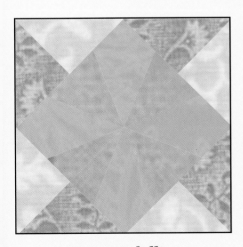

Cross Medallion

Cut-off Pinwheel

Diamond

Diamonds in the Square

Dimensional Diamonds

Divided Octagon

Dog-eared Cabin

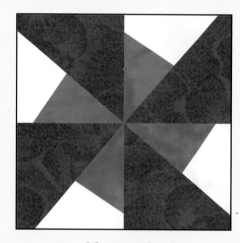

Double Pinwheel 1

Double Pinwheel 2

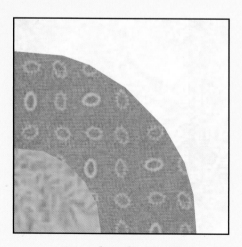

Drunkard's Trail

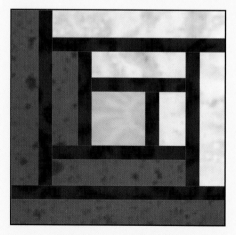

Edged Log Cabin

Fancy Triangles

Floating Cabins

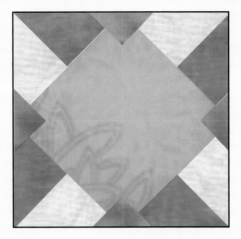

Flying Disk

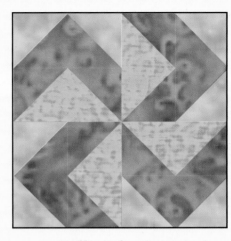

Follow the Geese

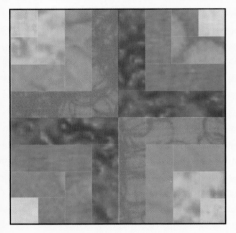

Four Corners Log Cabin

Four Corners 2

Four-Patch Corners

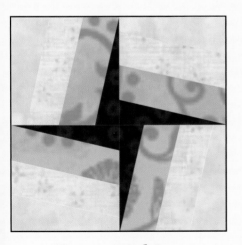

Four-pointed Star

Game Board

Grandmother's Fan

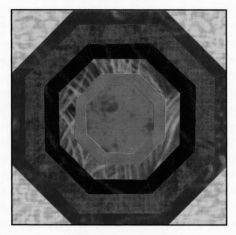

Hexagon Jewel

Hexagon

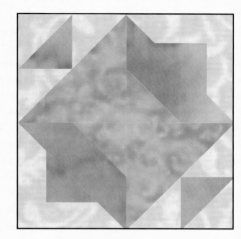

Hidden Flowers

Hugs and Kisses

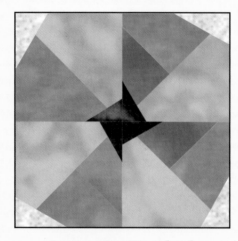

Interesting Pinwheel

Interlocking

Linked Squares

Log Cabin Askew

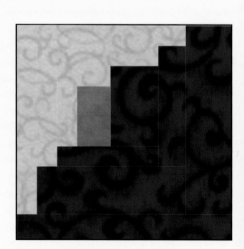

Log Cabin Curve

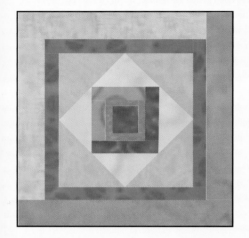

Log Cabin in a Log Cabin

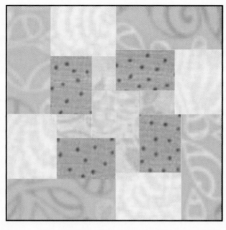

Log Cabin Quarters

Log Cabin Square

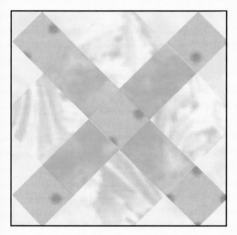

Lots of Squares

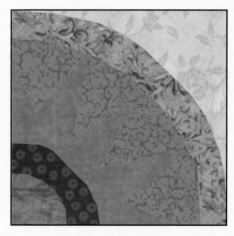

Medallion

Meeting of Geese

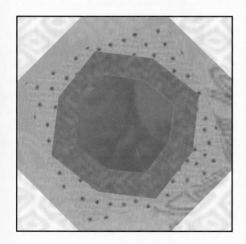

Octagon Surprise

Opposite Directions

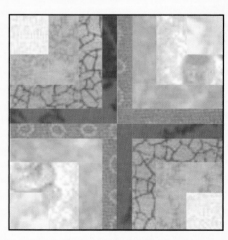

Outer Cabins

Partial Hearts

Pentagon

Pinwheel Geese

Plaid

Prism

Reverse Colors

Ribbon Heart

Ribbon Pinwheel

Ribbon-wrapped Block

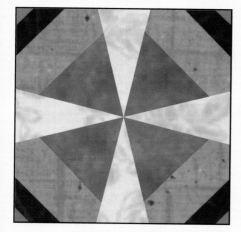

Rolling Tops

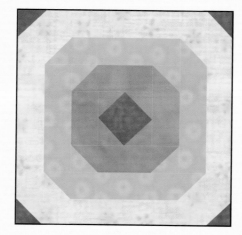

Rounded Cabin

See-through Star

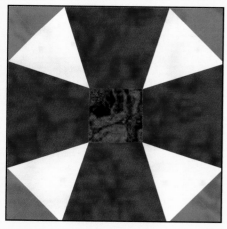

Simple Cross

Simple Flying Geese

Six-sided Pinwheel

Skinny Star

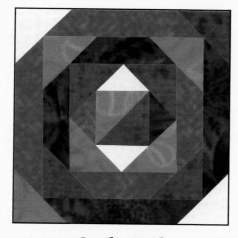

Snail's Trail

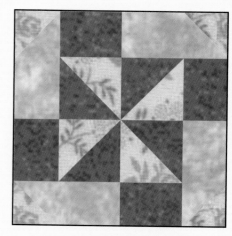

Snowball Pinwheel

So Easy Star

Square in a Square

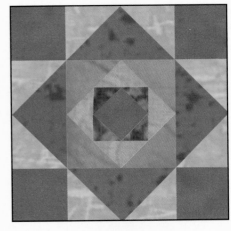

Stacked Squares 1

Stacked Squares 2

Star and Cross

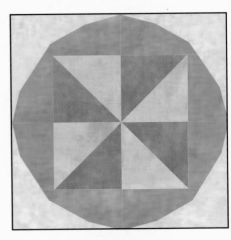

Star Balloon

Star Elegance

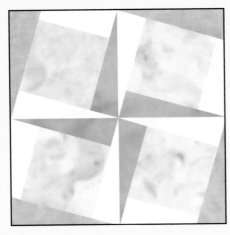

Star in a Box 3

Step Log Cabin

Stretched Pineapple

Striped Snowball

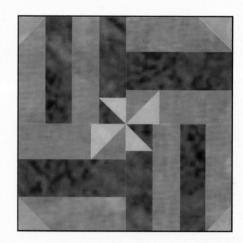

Striped Surprise 1

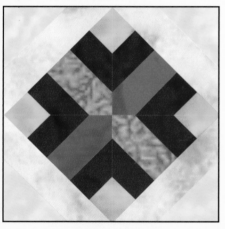

Striped Surprise 2

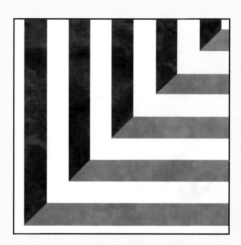

Stripes

Surprise Block

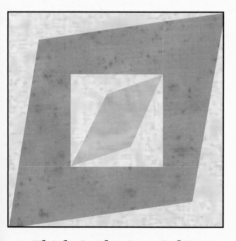

Thick Angles Log Cabin

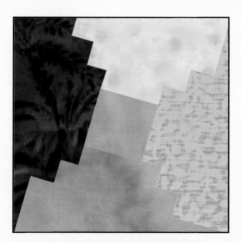

Tilted Log Cabin

Tipsy Cabin

Tumbling Triangles

Two-way Geese

Uneven Log Cabin

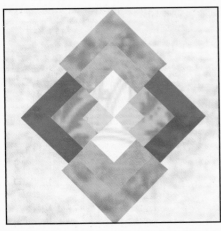

Uneven Log Cabins

Uneven Nine Patch

Unknown Block 1

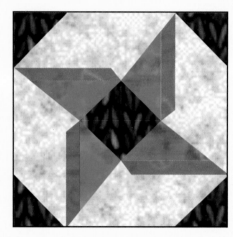

Unknown Block 2

Which Way

Woven Pinwheels

Zigzagging

General Directions

There are two different types of blocks in this book: blocks that use templates and blocks that use foundation or paper piecing. Whatever method you use, it is important to familiarize yourself with some basic general quiltmaking instructions.

FABRIC

For several hundred years, quilts were made with 100% cotton fabric, and this remains today the fabric of choice for most quilters.

There are many properties in cotton that make it especially well-suited to quiltmaking. There is less distortion in cotton fabric, thereby affording the quilter greater security in making certain that even the smallest bits of fabric will fit together. Because a quilt block made of cotton can be ironed flat with a steam iron, a puckered area, created by mistake can easily be fixed.

For years quilters were advised to prewash all of their fabric to test for colorfastness and shrinkage. Now most quilters don't bother to prewash, but they do pre-test. Cut a strip about 2″ wide from each piece of fabric that you will use in your quilt. Measure both the length and the width of the strip. Then immerse the strip in a bowl of very hot water, using a separate bowl for each piece of fabric. If your fabric bleeds, you may want to eliminate it.

Take each one of the strips and iron them dry using a very hot iron. Now measure them and compare them to the original strip. If all of the fabric is shrinking the same amount, there will be no problem. If some of the fabrics are shrinking and some are not, you will have to wash all of your fabric before beginning,

If you are never planning to wash your quilt, if your quilt is intended to be a wall-hanging, you could eliminate the pre-testing process. You may run the risk, however, of some future relative to whom you have willed your quilts, deciding that the wall hanging needs freshening up by washing.

Before beginning your quilt, make sure that your fabric is absolutely square. If it is not, you may have difficulty cutting square pieces. Fabric is woven with a crosswise and a lengthwise thread. Lengthwise threads should be parallel to the selvage (that's the finished edge along the sides; sometimes the fabric company prints its name along the selvage), and crosswise threads should be perpendicular to the selvage. If the fabric is off-grain, you can straighten it by gently pulling on the true bias in the opposite direction to the off-grain edge.

Whether you decide to make a quilt with templates or by foundation piecing, when you have finished making your blocks, follow the instructions on pages 124 to 128 for Finishing Your Quilt.

MAKING BLOCKS WITH TEMPLATES

All of the blocks on pages 4 through 69 are made using templates. All you need to do is to decide which block you would like to make.

You can print out the templates of your choice from the CD in the front of this book. **(Diagram 1)**

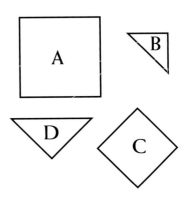

Diagram 1

116

Note: *If you are machine piecing, add a ¼" seam allowance all the way around the template.* **(Diagram 2)**

Diagram 2

Then glue the templates onto plastic or heavy cardboard. When you are certain that your glue has dried, cut out your templates. If your templates become worn, simply repeat the process. The blocks on the CD range in size from 4" to 15" square (depending on which type of block you are making), which are sizes that will fit on a regular sheet of paper. For those that are larger than an 8½" x 11" sheet of paper, you may need to go to your local copier store to print the blocks on 11" x 17" paper, See Frequently Asked Questions on the CD for guidelines on printing blocks over 8" square.

Cutting and Sewing for Machine Piecing

Lay the template (with the seam allowance already added) on the wrong side of the fabric near the top left edge of the material but not on the selvage, placing it so that as many straight sides of the piece as possible are parallel to the crosswise and lengthwise grain of the fabric. Trace around the template with a marking tool such as a hard lead pencil. This will be your cutting line; use a sharp scissors or a rotary cutter and cut accurately.

The traditional seam allowance in quilting is ¼" so be certain that you sew each seam with a ¼" seam allowance. After you have joined two pieces together, press the seams flat to one side, not open.

Cutting and Sewing for Hand Piecing

Lay the template on the fabric as described above for Machine Piecing and trace around it with your marking tool. This will be your stitching line. **(Diagram 3)**

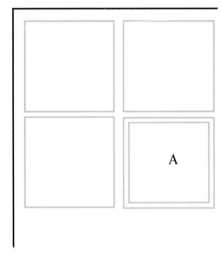

Diagram 3

Now measure ¼" around this shape. Using a ruler draw this second line. This is the line you will cut on. The seam allowance does not have to be perfect as it will not show, but the sewing line must be perfectly straight or the pieces will not fit together.

Hint: *Keep cut pieces in a labeled recloseable plastic bag.*

117

FOUNDATION PIECING

Materials

Before you begin, decide the kind of foundation on which you are planning to piece the blocks.

Since the blocks in this book are printed from a CD using your computer and printer, the most popular choice for a foundation is regular copy paper since it is readily available. You can also use freezer paper. It comes in sheets by C. Jenkins or a roll by Reynolds®. If you use the roll, you will have to cut sheets that will fit through your printer. If using freezer paper, be sure to print the pattern on the dull side. Then as you piece, use a small craft iron or a travel iron to press fabric pieces in place on the foundation after sewing each seam. The paper is removed once the blocks are completely sewn.

There are other options for foundation materials that can be used with your computer and printer. One type is Tear Away™ or Fun-dation™, translucent non-woven materials, combining the advantages of both paper and fabric. They are easy to see through, and like paper, they can be removed with ease. Another foundation material is one that dissolves in water after use called Dissolve Away Foundation Paper by EZ Quilting®.

Preparing the Foundation

Since the Block Patterns are given in several sizes on a CD, preparing your foundation is easier than ever. All you need to do is decide which block you would like to make (from 2" to 8" square) and which size you will need for your quilt. Place the CD in your computer, choose the block and print the number of copies that you will need for your quilt.

The blocks on the CD range in size from 4" to 12" square since those are the sizes that will fit on a regular sheet of paper. For those that are larger than

an 8½" x 11" sheet of paper, you may need to go to your local copier store to print the blocks on 11" x 17" paper. See Frequently Asked Questions on the CD for guidelines on printing blocks over 8" square.

Cutting the Fabric

In foundation piecing, you do not have to cut perfect shapes! You can, therefore, use odd pieces of fabric: squares, strips, and rectangles. The one thing you must remember, however, is that every piece must be at least ¼" larger on all sides than the space it is going to cover. Strips and squares are easy: just measure the length and width of the needed space and add ½" all around. Cut your strip to that measurement. Triangles, however, can be a bit tricky. In that case, measure the widest point of the triangle and cut your fabric about ½" to 1" wider.

Other Supplies for Foundation Piecing

You will need a cleaned and oiled sewing machine, glue stick, pins, paper scissors, fabric scissors, and foundation material.

Before beginning to sew your actual block by machine, determine the proper stitch length. Use a piece of the paper you are planning to use for the foundation and draw a straight line on it. Set your machine so that it sews with a fairly short stitch (about 20 stitches per inch). Sew along the line. If you can tear the paper apart with ease, you are sewing with the right length. You don't want to sew with such a short stitch that the paper falls apart by itself.

Using a Pattern

The numbers on the block show the order in which the pieces are to be placed and sewn on the foundation. It is extremely important that you follow the numbers; otherwise the entire process won't work. The letters refer to the sections that need to be cut apart in order to sew the block. The sections are divided by bold lines. Cut along the bold lines to separate the pattern sections before sewing. Refer to the photo on the pattern page for fabric color placement.

Making the Block

The important thing to remember about making a foundation block is that the fabric goes on the unmarked side of the foundation while you sew on the printed side. The finished block is a mirror image of the original pattern.

Step 1: Hold the foundation up to a light source—even a window—with the unmarked side facing you. Find the space marked 1 on the unmarked side and put a dab of glue there. Place the fabric right side up on the unmarked side on Space 1, making certain that the fabric overlaps at least ¼" on all sides of space 1. **(Diagram 4)**

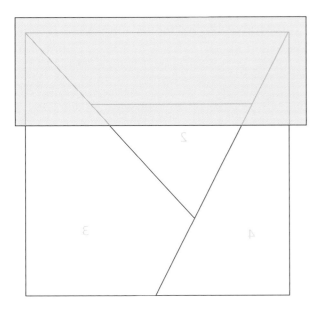

Diagram 4

Step 2: Fold the foundation along the line between Space 1 and Space 2. Cut the fabric so that it is ¼" from the fold. **(Diagram 5)**

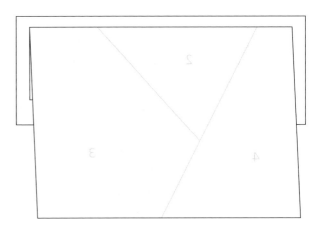

Diagram 5

Step 3: With right sides together, place Fabric Piece 2 on Fabric Piece 1, making sure that the edge of Piece 2 is even with the just-trimmed edge of Piece 1. **(Diagram 6)**

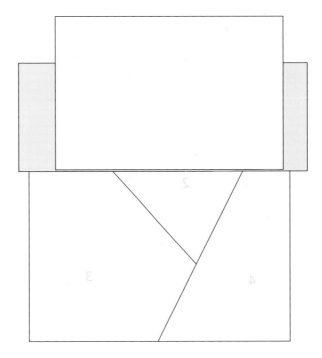

Diagram 6

119

Step 4: To make certain that Piece 2 will cover Space 2, fold the fabric piece back along the line between Space 1 and Space 2. **(Diagram 7)**

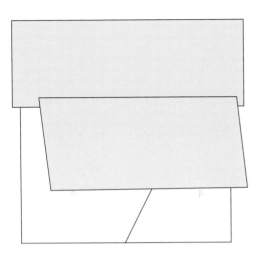

Diagram 7

Step 5: With the marked side of the foundation facing up, place the piece on the sewing machine (or sew by hand), holding both Piece 1 and Piece 2 in place. Sew along the line between Space 1 and Space 2. **(Diagram 8)**

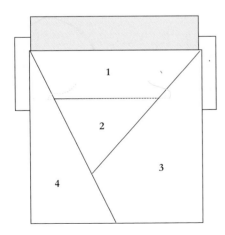

Diagram 8

Step 6: Turn the work over and open Piece 2. Press open. **(Diagram 9)**

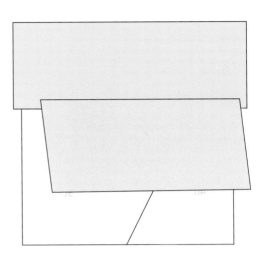

Diagram 9

Step 7: Turning the work so that the marked side is on top, fold the foundation forward along the line between Space 1+2 and Space 3. Trim about ⅛" to ¼" from the fold. It is easier to trim the fabric if you pull the paper away from the stitching. If you use fabric as your foundation, fold the fabric forward as far as it will go and then start to trim. **(Diagram 10)**

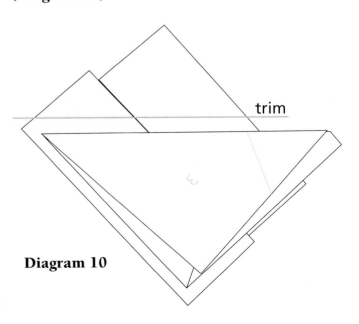

Diagram 10

Step 8: Place Fabric Piece 3 right side down even with the just-trimmed edge. **(Diagram 11)**

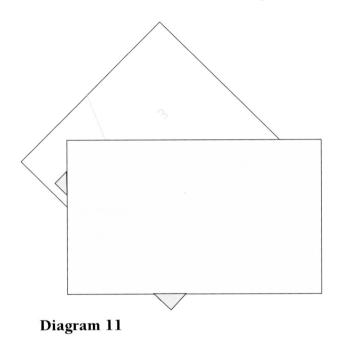

Diagram 11

Step 9: Turn the block over to the marked side and sew along the line between Space 1+2 and Space 3. **(Diagram 12)**

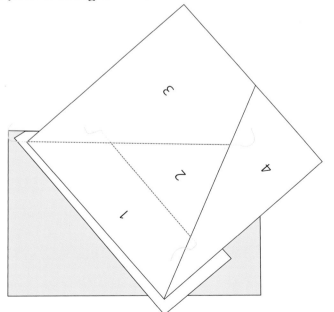

Diagram 12

Step 10: Turn the work over, open Piece 3 and press open. **(Diagram 13)**

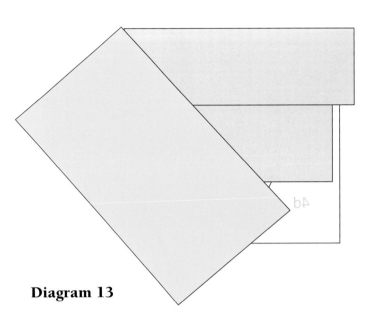

Diagram 13

Step 11: In the same way you have added the other pieces, add Piece #4 to complete this block. Trim the fabric ¼" from the edge of the foundation. The foundation-pieced block is completed. **(Diagram 14)**

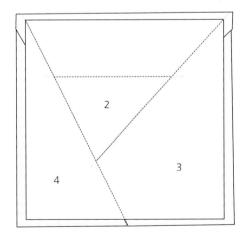

Diagram 14

Note: *The finished block is a mirror image to the pattern used to complete the sewing.*

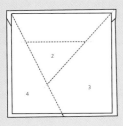
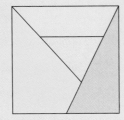

After you have finished sewing a block, don't immediately remove the paper. Since you are often piecing with tiny bits of fabric, grainline is not a factor. Therefore, some of the pieces may have been cut on the bias and may have a tendency to stretch. You can eliminate any problem with distortion by keeping the paper in place until all of the blocks have been sewn together. If, however, you want to remove the paper, stay stitch along the outer edge of the block to help keep the block in shape.

Sewing Multiple Sections

Many of the blocks in foundation piecing are created with two or more sections. These sections, which are indicated by letters, are individually pieced and then sewn together. The cutting line for these sections is indicated by a bold line. Before you start to make any of these multi-section blocks, begin by cutting the foundation piece apart so that each section is worked independently.

Note: Be sure to leave a ¹⁄₄″ seam allowance around each section.

Step 1: Following the previous instructions for Making the Block, complete each section. Then place the sections right sides together. Pin the corners of the top section to the corners of the bottom section. **(Diagram 15)**

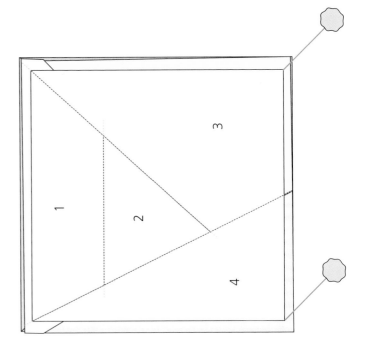

Diagram 15

Step 2: When you are certain that the pieces are aligned correctly, sew the two sections together using the regular stitch length on the sewing machine.

Step 3: Press the sections open and continue sewing the sections in pairs. **(Diagram 16)**

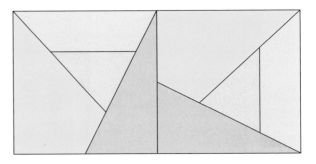

Diagram 16

Step 4: Sew necessary pairs of sections together to complete the block. **(Diagram 17)**

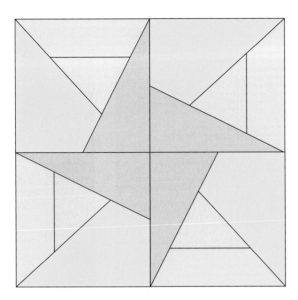

Diagram 17

What You Don't Want to Forget

1. If you plan to sew by hand, begin by taking some backstitches that will anchor the thread at the beginning of the line. Then use a backstitch every four or five stitches. End the stitching with a few backstitches.

2. If you plan to sew by machine, start stitching two or three stitches before the start of the stitching line and finish your stitching two or three stitches beyond the end.

3. Use a short stitch (about 20 stitches per inch) for paper foundations to make it easier to remove the paper. If the paper falls apart as you sew, your stitches are too short.

4. Press each seam as you finish it.

5. Stitching which goes from a space into another space will not interfere with adding additional fabric pieces.

6. Remember to trim all seam allowances at least ¼".

7. When sewing points, start from the wide end and sew towards the point.

8. Unless you plan to use it only once in the block, it is a good idea to stay away from directional prints in foundation piecing.

9. When cutting pieces for foundation piecing, never worry about the grainline.

10. Always remember to sew on the marked side, placing the fabric on the unmarked side.

11. Follow the numerical order, or it won't work.

12. Once you have finished making a block do not remove the paper until the entire quilt has been finished unless you stay stitch around the outside of the block.

13. Be sure that the ink you use to make your foundation is permanent and will not wash out into your fabric.

FINISHING YOUR QUILT

Simple Borders

To add your borders, measure the quilt top lengthwise and cut two border strips to that length by the width measurement given in the instructions. Strips may have to be pieced to achieve the correct length.

To make the joining seam less noticeable, sew the strips together diagonally. Place two strips right sides together at right angles. Sew a diagonal seam. **(Diagram 18)**

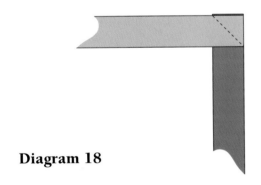

Diagram 18

Trim excess fabric ¼" from stitching. **(Diagram 19)**

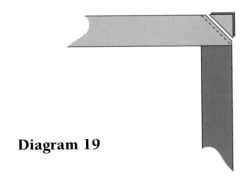

Diagram 19

Press seam open. **(Diagram 20)**

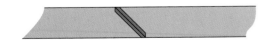

Diagram 20

Sew strips to the sides of the quilt. Press toward border. Now measure the quilt top crosswise, being sure to include the borders you have just added. Cut two border strips to that length, following the width measurement given in the instructions.

Add these borders to the top and bottom of the quilt.

Repeat this process for any additional borders. Use the ¼" seam allowance at all times and press all of the seams toward the border just added. Press the quilt top carefully.

Attaching the Batting and Backing

There are a number of different types of batting on the market today including the new fusible battings that eliminate the need for basting. Your choice of batting will depend upon how you are planning to use your quilt. If the quilt is to serve as a wall hanging, you will probably want to use a thin cotton batting. A quilt made with a thin cotton or cotton/polyester blend works best for machine quilting. Very thick polyester batting should be used only for tied quilts.

The best fabric for quilt backing is 100% cotton fabric. If your quilt is larger than the available fabric, you will have to piece your backing fabric. When joining the fabric, try not to have a seam going down the center. Instead cut off the selvages and make a center strip that is about 36" wide and have narrower strips at the sides. Seam the pieces together and carefully iron the seams open. (This is one of the few times in making a quilt that a seam should be pressed open.) Several fabric manufacturers are now selling fabric in 90" or 108"-widths for use as backing fabric.

It is a good idea to remove the batting from its wrapping 24 hours before you plan to use it and open it out to full size. You will find that the batting will now lie flat when you are ready to use it.

The batting and the backing should be cut about one to two inches larger on all sides than the quilt top. Place the backing wrong side up on a flat surface. Smooth out the batting on top of this, matching the outer edges. Center the quilt top, right side up, on top of the batting.

Now the quilt layers must be held together before quilting, and there are several methods for doing this:

Safety-pin Basting: Starting from the center and working toward the edges, pin through all layers at one time with large safety pins. The pins should be placed no more than 4" apart. As you work, think of your quilting plan to make sure that the pins will avoid prospective quilting lines.

Thread Basting: Baste the three layers together with long stitches. Start in the center and sew toward the edges in a number of diagonal lines.

Quilt-gun Basting: This handy trigger tool pushes nylon tags through all layers of the quilt. Start in the center and work toward the outside edges. The tags should be placed about 4" apart. You can sew right over the tags, which can then be easily removed by cutting them off with scissors.

Spray or Heat-set Basting: Several manufacturers have spray adhesives available especially for quilters. Apply these products by following the manufacturers' directions. You might want to test these products before you use them to make sure that they meet your requirements.

Fusible Iron-on Batting: These battings are a wonderful new way to hold quilt layers together without using any of the other time-consuming methods of basting. Again, you will want to test these battings to be certain that you are happy with the results. Follow the manufacturers' directions.

Quilting

If you like the process of hand quilting, you can—of course—finish these projects by hand quilting. However, if you want to finish these quilts quickly, you might want to use a sewing machine for quilting.

If you have never used a sewing machine for quilting, you may want to find a book and read about the technique. You do not need a special machine for quilting. Just make sure that your machine has been oiled and is in good working condition.

If you are going to do machine quilting, you should invest in an even-feed foot. This foot is designed to feed the top and bottom layers of a quilt evenly through the machine. The foot prevents puckers from forming as you machine quilt. Use a fine transparent nylon thread or thread that matches the background in the top and regular sewing thread in the bobbin.

Quilting in the ditch is one of the easiest ways to machine quilt. This is a term used to describe stitching along the seam line between two pieces of fabric. Using your fingers, pull the blocks or pieces apart slightly and machine stitch right between the two pieces. The stitching will look better if you keep the stitching to the side of the seam that does not have the extra bulk of the seam under it. The quilting will be hidden in the seam.

Free-form machine quilting can be used to quilt around a design or to quilt a motif. The quilting is done with a darning foot and the feed dogs down on the sewing machine. It takes practice to master free-form quilting because you are controlling the movement of the quilt under the needle rather than the sewing machine moving the quilt. You can quilt in any direction – up and down, side-to-side, and even in circles – without pivoting the quilt around the needle. Practice this quilting method before trying it on your quilt.

Attaching the Continuous Machine Binding

Once the quilt has been quilted, it must be bound to cover the raw edges.

Step 1: Start by trimming the backing and batting even with the quilt top. Measure the quilt top and cut enough 2½"-wide strips to go around all four sides of the quilt plus 12". Join the strips end to end with diagonal seams and trim the corners. Press the seams open. **(Diagram 21)**

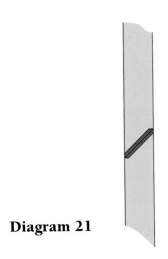

Diagram 21

Step 2: Cut one end of the strip at a 45-degree angle and press under ¼". **(Diagram 22)**

Diagram 22

Step 3: Press entire strip in half lengthwise, wrong sides together. **(Diagram 23)**

Diagram 23

Step 4: On the back of the quilt, position the binding in the middle of one side, keeping the raw edges together. Sew the binding to the quilt with the ¼" seam allowance, beginning about three inches below the folded end of the binding. At the corner, stop ¼" from the edge of the quilt and backstitch. **(Diagram 24)**

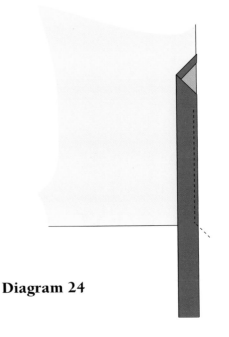

Diagram 24